The Way It Was In Appalachia

Geraldine Oxford-Tolliver

authorHOUSE®

AuthorHouse™
1663 Liberty Drive, Suite 200
Bloomington, IN 47403
www.authorhouse.com
Phone: 1-800-839-8640

First published by AuthorHouse 2/3/2009

ISBN: 978-1-4389-0846-5 (sc)

Printed in the United States of America
Bloomington, Indiana

This book is printed on acid-free paper.

Acknowledgment

In Loving Memory of My Mother
Ida Tolliver

Born May 21, 1905 in Greenup County, Kentucky
Died August 27, 1944 and buried in Dunham Cemetery, Jenkins, Kentucky

A woman friend in St. Louis, Missouri - Judy Stanforth told me, "You have an interesting life, you should write about it."

The tutor that I had in St. Louis - Torrie Sanders said, when I mentioned the fact about my writing mechanics not being that good, "Don't worry about it. They will take care of the language."

Richard Ponto, my loving husband of 36 years, who, when I said to him, "I don't know how to write this," replied, "Just tell it like it was."

Sharon Harris-Powers, my daughter. I thank her for typing all the handwritten pages, trying to make some sense of it all, and for the encouragement she has provided as together we have wrote this, my life's story.

John Russell, Geraldine, Clarence King Jr. (Chuck) and Sharon Kay

---

Geraldine Tolliver-Oxford-Ponto

Today Geraldine is about to turn 85 young years old. She has had a full life, never experiencing a dull moment. She has laughed, cried, loved, through good times and bad. She has endured the bad times, and surely enjoyed the good times. She loves to dance. If she could come back in another life, she would love to be a "New York Rockettte."

She watches television is thankful she lives in America, and proud of her Southern heritage. She reads countless books with her newfound education, travels more than the average person, and thinks St. Louis; Missouri is the greatest place with its magnificent Arch.

Her children, grandchildren, great-grandchildren, nieces and nephews love her deeply. She has excellent health, and the most beautiful smile. Her disposition is always upbeat, and she is very pleasant to keep company with.

She is active in life, which probably accounts for her good health and mental well-being.

Contents

Chapter One	*Hillbillies*	1
Chapter Two	*The Bear*	3
Chapter Three	*The Mountains of Kentucky*	4
Chapter Four	*Early Childhood*	7
Chapter Five	*Diphtheria*	9
Chapter Six	*The Aunts and the Uncles*	11
Chapter Seven	*Father*	17
Chapter Eight	*Mother*	22
Chapter Nine	*The Scrappers*	27
Chapter Ten	*The "Moonshine" Years*	30
Chapter Eleven	*The Coal Mines*	33
Chapter Twelve	*The "White Castle" Kid*	36
Chapter Thirteen	*Segregation*	37
Chapter Fourteen	*Third Grade*	39
Chapter Fifteen	*Nostalgia*	42
Chapter Sixteen	*The Honey Wagon*	45
Chapter Seventeen	*The Thirties*	47
Chapter Eighteen	*Clarence King Morefield Sr.*	49
Chapter Nineteen	*California*	53
Chapter Twenty	*Idaho*	55
Chapter Twenty-One	*The Arrival of Chuck*	56
Chapter Twenty-Two	*The Trip Home*	58
Chapter Twenty-Three	*Back Home with Chuck*	61
Chapter Twenty-Four	*After the War*	64
Chapter Twenty-Five	*The First Years in West Virginia*	68
Chapter Twenty-Six	*The Boys*	72
Chapter Twenty-Seven	*On the Move, Again*	75
Chapter Twenty-Eight	*The Early Years in Detroit*	78
Chapter Twenty-Nine	*Hillbillies and City Slickers*	81
Chapter Thirty	*The Next Move*	84
Chapter Thirty- *One*	*The Car*	86
Chapter Thirty-Two	*John's Trip to Belle Isle*	88
Chapter Thirty-Three	*Babies*	89
Chapter Thirty-Four	*Hudson's*	91

Chapter Thirty-Five	*Sharon Is Born*	96
Chapter Thirty-SixThe	*Old House on Campbell*	98
Chapter Thirty-Seven	*Henley Place*	100
Chapter Thirty Eight	*Lexington Avenue*	105
Chapter Thirty Nine	*Two More Moves*	107
Chapter Forty	*The End of My Life with Clarence*	110
Chapter Forty-One	*Richard Ponto Comes/Bootsy Leaves*	113
Chapter Forty Two	*Dedicated to Bootsy and Herbert*	116
Chapter Forty-Three	*Dedicated to Gloria Ann, "Cat"*	119
EPILOGUE		121
Editor's Note		129

Additional Chapters of Heritage and Historical Accounts

Chapter Forty Four	*The Tolliver Vendetta*	132
Chapter Forty Five	*Bad John Wright*	165
Chapter Forty-Six	*They Built a Town*	168
Chapter Forty-Seven	*History of Taillefer/Taliaferro/Tolliver*	171
Chapter Forty-Eight	*Origin of the Taliaferro Name Published BeliefsAndFamily Traditions*	173
Chapter Forty-Nine	*The Counts of Angouleme - And Isabelle Taillefer*	175
Chapter Fifty	*A Brief Sketch of the Counts of Angouleme*	176
Chapter Fifty	*OneIsabelle Taillefer and King John of England*	178
Chapter Fifty Two	*The Barbarian and Julius Caesar*	180
Chapter Fifty-Three	*Bartholomew Taliaferro of England*	181
Chapter Fifty Four	*John Taliaferro Toliver*	183
Chapter Fifty FiveJohn	*Oxford*	184
Chapter Fifty-Six	*Descendants of William Oxford*	188

Chapter One
Hillbillies

I never have minded being called one of them "Hillbillies" because I always knew there were worse people in the world. Our ancestors were among some of the first prominent people to settle in the Cumberland Mountains in the early 1700's. They were the Taliaferro's.

Tolliver is a corruption of Taliaferro. We have found, from doing genealogy, there was a Captain Francis Taliafero in 1763 in Fredericksburg, Virginia and a mention of a General Lawrence Taliafero in Orange County, Virginia in 1765. Our mother told us that she had been told that the name had been changed at Ellis Island.

When she told us, we never believed her. We said, "No way! We don't have any Italian blood!" Truth is we must. 'Cause the name Taliaferro sounds about as Italian as it gets.

John Fox wrote about the Tollivers in "The Trail of the Lonesome Pines." He wrote that the Tollivers were of good blood, that they came from North Carolina and Eastern Virginia that the men were tall, had black curly hair and black eyes, were hard working people, and always had land of their own. They sold the land that had coal on it to the mining companies. The ones I was lucky enough to meet were friendly and always smiling. A lot of them settled in the area of Millstone, Thornton, and Rock House, Kentucky. At one time there were so many Tollivers in that area that it was called "Tolliver Town."

I have a picture of my Great Grandfather - Remington Winston Tolliver. I look at it to see what I could tell about him. He looks like a nice looking, young man. I could see that some of his features were passed along to my mother, even though she never looked anything like her father, at least not in the pictures I've seen.

We do not have a picture of her mother, but I remember seeing one at one time, and I remember she was a pretty woman.

Everyone who knew our mother would tell us how pretty she was, and they must have been right, because after us girls grew up, we weren't bad to look at either. One of us won a beauty contest (Magdalene). We all have great legs and mother always said mine were just like hers. My sister, Beatrice, had the most beautiful head of natural curly hair. Her nickname came from a comic strip in the paper called, "Boots and Her Buddies" because she looked like Boots.

My claim to fame is my handwriting. Several other people in my family have good handwriting, too, and in some of the writings of my grandfathers you can see where it comes from.

Our genes have carried over into our children. I wouldn't say any of us girls were beautiful, but I can truthfully say that some of our girls, our granddaughters, and our great-granddaughters are. We also have very good-looking sons, grandsons, and great-grandsons.

We have never rejected our mountain heritage. The Tollivers have worked hard to better themselves. I don't mind being called a "Hillbilly". But it's the tone of voice that is used, and who makes the remark that can hurt or make me angry.

I do know that my ancestors on both sides of my parents' families were among the first settlers in Kentucky and Virginia, and as I have gotten older I have become proud to be from the mountains.

Chapter Two
The Bear

When we were just small children, our mother would tell us this story about our Grandmother and Grandfather. It took place when she was just a small child, herself.

Charley Tolliver, her father, had built a log cabin with the help of some other men. The cabin was all finished, except for the floor. They had laid a foundation, made out of timbers, and were going to nail floorboards on top of the timbers to make the floor solid.

But before they could do that, the men had to go away and they left my mother alone in the house with her mother, Elizabeth Bentley Tolliver.

That day they had butchered a hog.

Elizabeth decided to cut some pieces of meat for them to roast over the fire in the fireplace.

While they were roasting the meat, a bear wandered up under the house, and started trying to push its head up through the loose floorboards. The bear was trying to get into the house because it was hungry and could smell the meat roasting on the fire.

My grandmother got a hatchet, and every time the bear would stick its ugly head up through the crack in the flooring, she would swing that hatchet, and chop it on its head. They were afraid for their very lives. After a while the bear stopped, and it got real quiet.

The next day, when the men came back, Elizabeth told them of the horrors of the night before. The men took off hunting for the bear in the woods, and finally found it lying dead and covered with blood.

When we asked her what they did with the bear, she would say, "We ate it, and it was very tasty."

Chapter Three
The Mountains of Kentucky

The day I was born my mother, Ida Tolliver (Taliaferro), always loved to tell a story about that day. She had planted some lettuce, and it had begun to snow. She had my father, James Ray Oxford Sr., take a sheet and go out and cover up her lettuce so the snow wouldn't fall on it.

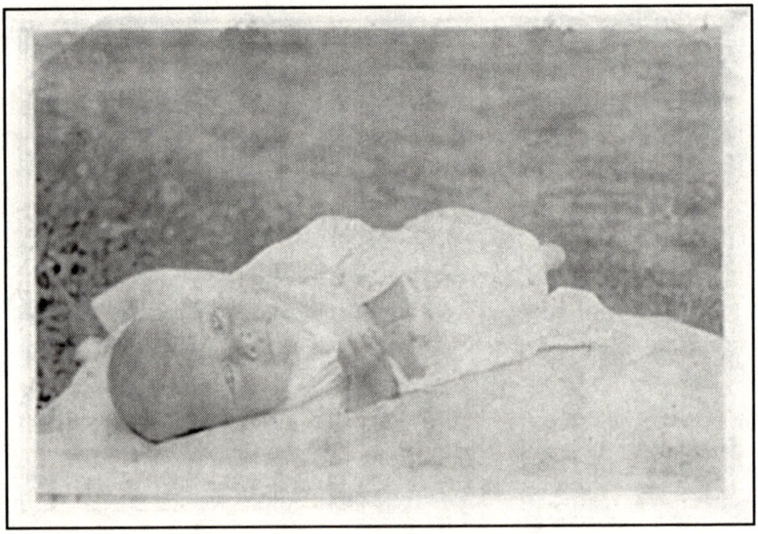

Geraldine Oxford, born May 6, 1923 in Greasy Creek, Kentucky

She said a family named Sanders was sitting on their front porch, swinging in a swing. That seemed to be a strange coincidence when, years later, my baby sister, Gloria Ann, married one of their sons, Tommie Sanders, and they had a son named Gregory Allen Sanders.

We grew up in the mountains of Kentucky, in a town called Dunham. We spent most of our time up in the hills playing. We would build playhouses, using rocks. We would make tables, beds, and chairs, finding a long rock to wrap up in a cloth for a baby, and gathering small rocks to outline the outside of our playhouse.

We would gather acorns, and use the shells for cups. We ate what was in season: ripe paw paws, apples, nuts, sour grass gooseberries, and we used grapevines to swing on. We would stay up in the mountains all day, climbing up to the tops, and sometimes going down the other side into other small towns.

Jenkins is a part of the Appalachian Mountains. It is nice. You could even say it is a beautiful place, all according to how you looked at it. The hills all around the area had many different trees: maple, birch, walnut, flowering dogwoods, wild honey suckle and mountain laurel. And then, there were the wildflowers. The one I liked best was called Indian Paint. It was a red-colored bush. In the spring it is great, but when fall came, the colors of the foliage were just beautiful.

"God's paint brush," I heard people call it.

Up the mountain there is a place called Raven Rock, a scenic look out on the way to Pound, Virginia. Everyone loved to go there. You can see the town and Jenkins Lake from up there. In the winter when it snowed, the mountains were beautiful, covered in white. But the winters were never really cold.

Jenkins Lake is nice. It was the place to go and the thing to do – to take a walk on "Lakeside" to look at the homes and the lake – in "small town" USA.

You would always meet people you knew who were there doing the same things. On the upper side of the lake was a ballpark. It was right up close to the mountains. On the 4th of July they would always be a baseball game. Parents would take their kids up the sides of the mountains and play together, and they could still look over the park and take-in the game. We would have a great time. Watermelons in galvanized tubs filled with ice, Nehi soda pop to drink, and hot dogs on sticks to roast along with gooey marshmallows.

The children could run and play freely. I am sure our parents didn't worry about us. There were no strangers, no liquor or beer. Jenkins is part of a dry county. If you wanted anything to drink, you had to go to Virginia to get it.

The mountains were our playgrounds. We knew where the snakes were and we stayed away from those places. We knew where streams of water were and they were always clear and cold. Sometimes there would be leaves floating in the streams. We would pick them out and drink the cool water from them.

What was really unusual was, we always took my baby sister, Gloria Ann, with us. And I mean she was a real "baby" baby. We carried her everywhere we went. I guess our mother knew she was safe with us, for I loved her dearly.

The only thing that ever happened to her was once, when we were playing in a creek (she was able to stand up by then). We stood her on a rock that wasn't level and it tilted her over, head first, into a pool of water deep enough to cover her completely. I remember grasping her by her diaper and pulling her up, wiping the water off her face, and then taking her home.

Later, when telling our mother what had happened, mother said, "Oh, my poor baby, you're going to drown her."

I don't know how old I was when we stopped going up into the mountains. I do know, during my teen years, my brother, Jim, was still going up into them. He had a rifle and shotgun, and he would go hunting. I use to really worry about him. I'd ask my mother, "Aren't you worried?" And she would say, "No, he will be all right."

Jim would take other boys that were friends of his with him. They would go up on the mountain behind our house, in a place called Barn Hill. Sometimes one of the boys he would take with him would get scared, and Jim would have to bring him back down. The language he used was something else.

He would make it plain that they wouldn't get to go back ever again. One of the names he would call them was, "coward", saying they were afraid of the dark, and their own shadow. He enjoyed going into the mountains at night. He'd take potatoes to roast on the fire, and corn, and he'd stay out all night. Sometimes he would kill rabbits and groundhogs and bring them back home.

One time he killed the biggest groundhog I had ever seen, and skinned it, himself. Our mother wanted to cook it. After he finished skinning it, it still had hairs clinging to its skin. Our mother made us girls pick all the hairs off, which we didn't want to do. To us it was the most awful looking thing we have ever seen - big, fat, and red.

After we got the hairs off, we put it in a pan, salted and peppered the meat real good, and put it in the oven.

After it roasted for a while, it started smelling real good. When it was done, we sat it out on top of the stove and started picking off pieces of meat to taste. It was delicious actually; Jim came in the kitchen, and caught us. He started yelling, telling our mother we were eating the ground hog, and for her to make us stop, which she did.

She would say, "Now you girls leave that groundhog alone. You didn't want to fix it for your brother, so leave it alone." He took it up to our mother's room and the two of them ate it.

Chapter Four
Early Childhood

In 1927 when I was just four years old, out playing in the yard, I remember seeing my mother and another woman standing on the porch of the house where we lived. They both had on aprons and their hair was tied up in cloths, which were always one of the babies' diapers.

They were standing with their arms folded, looking up at the sky saying, "This is the day Lindbergh is going to fly over."

I played out in the yard all day, watching and waiting for him to fly over.

One of my fondest memories of my mother was in 1928. She was making herself a dress of Swiss dots with roses on it and she made me one, too. I was about five years old.

She and my father went to a square dance, and they took me with them. One of the songs, they sang and danced to, went like this, "Flies in the buttermilk, shoo fly, shoo. Flies in the sugar bowl, shoo fly, shoo." How can you forget a song like that?

The first Halloween, that I remember, I was coming to the house from outside playing and there was this frightening thing standing near the house. As a child you don't know what it is. It jumps at you and hollers, "BOO!" It scares you to death! You scream! Then the thing jerks the mask off, grabs you and hugs you tight, telling you "It's me, your mama!"

"Those Memories, How They Haunt Me," is the title of a song Dolly Parton sings. It makes me think a lot of my early childhood.

I lived in Virginia in 1929, with my mother, father, two sisters and a baby brother. I was only six years old, but I can remember my father leaving home early in the morning. It would still be dark when he left, and it would be dark again when he came home from working in the coalmines. He would be carrying a big lump of coal on his shoulder for our stove.

In 1930, the coal mines that my father worked for shut down and we moved to Kentucky. I was seven years old. It was in the fall of the year.

My mother always had a garden. I remember the biggest pumpkin and a galvanized tub full of mums being moved with us. They set the tub of mums on the back of the car, (where the trunk would be later), and put the pumpkin in the car with us children. It was an all day trip.

Now, when I go there to visit it takes just an hour to go the same distance.

Chapter Five
Diphtheria

In about 1925 or 1926, I got sick with diphtheria (which later turned into an epidemic). Thanks to my mother taking care of me, I was one of the few that lived through it. She would tell how she would put gauze around her finger and clean the mucus out of my throat.

Afterwards I had surgery for mastoid, damage to the inner ear bones. They removed the infected bone. What resulted was a lifetime of hearing loss and subsequent ear problems. When I complained to one of my doctors, he told me, "Most of the children who got diphtheria in the 1920's died."

That I surely had a mother who loved me and took good care of me."

One of the first memories I have when I got sick was of my father carrying me on his back going into the coalmines.

Some of the miners asked him, "Mr. Oxford, where are you going?" He answered,

"I'm taking her to the doctor in Jenkins."

We lived at McRoberts at that time, and he was taking the shortcut, under the mountains, and through the mineshafts that he worked in.

Another thing happened when I tried to get out of Jenkins Hospital and got caught by an orderly as I was going down the hill from where the hospital was located. He was a man of color and had a white jacket on. He asked me where I was going. I told him I was going to get an ice cream. He picked me up and took me back to the hospital.

My mother said they never did know how I got out of the bed without getting hurt.

Later we moved to Virginia. My father took me to Bristol to see a doctor for my ears. We were staying on the second floor of a hotel. I had gone to sleep and father went downstairs to the barbershop to get a haircut. I remember waking up and finding him gone.

I thought he had gone out, so I climbed out the window looking for him. I could see people down in the street. They were very upset. Within minutes my father was at the window telling me to come inside.

My mother told the story later.

It seems that between the hotel and the next building they had taken roofing paper and nailed it to each side of the building so the rain wouldn't fall into the alleyway. It was only the roofing paper that I was walking on. They never could figure out why it didn't tear.

Sometime after that, my mother took me to see a doctor in Norton. She wasn't allowed to come in the examination room with me. The doctor looked in my left ear, saw a piece of bone (left from my surgery), and tried to pull it out.

He was holding me between his legs and had a headlock on me. I was crying.

He was hurting me and wouldn't let me go. He kept telling me to "hold still."

The next time he picked at my ear, and hurt me, I bit his wrist as hard as I could. I screamed as I bit him, and he finally let me go. He took me back to my mother, waiting outside the room, and told her,

"Don't ever bring her back."

Some years later, I felt something on the back of my ear. It felt real sharp. Apparently the bone had worked itself loose. My mother took a needle, opened it up, and took it out. It was about the size of a grain of rice.

Chapter Six
The Aunts and the Uncles

My father's brother, John Oxford, lived in Big Stone Gap, Virginia most of his life. He lived to be 102 years old. I attended his 100th birthday party. I asked him if he remembered when he came up to Inman, Virginia to get me and take me home with him.

I was remembering how it was, and while I told him about it he was laughing and shaking his head up and down in agreement.

At the time, I was four or five and he was thirty-six or seven. He had no children of his own, but for some reason he liked me and called me "Jellyroll." It must have been because I was fat. The other pet name my father and he called me was "Dabber." My father called me "Dabber" for years.

The highway going to Uncle Johns in Big Stone Gap had a river alongside it, and we would travel down the road with me standing on the floor in the back of the car. He had a lever on the dashboard that pulled out, and when he pushed it back in it made a loud noise.

The noise made it feel like the car was going faster. I would hang onto the back seat and jump up and down yelling, "Do it again, Uncle John does it again!" I thought he was the greatest.

He would play that game with me until we would get to the house. (I have since spoken to the men in my family, and they say the old cars had what was called a "throttle" to regulate the gas intake. When my Uncle John pulled the lever in and out in his car it would make the motor race, and made it sound like it was going faster.)

Geraldine and her father James Ray Oxford Sr.
Illustrating the automobiles of that time period.

I loved going to Uncle John and Aunt Cindy's house. They had a porch; painted gray, with wicker furniture and a porch swing with pillows that would make me want to swing for hours. Inside, there were beautiful things that Aunt Cindy collected dishes and whatnots.

Everything was beautiful to look at. She loved colorful glass sitting in the sunlight.

There were shelves on the walls, full of plates and platters. She had every kind of Depression glass that was ever made. She also had an organ with pull knobs and a foot player, and all kinds of pictures. Some of them were from the First World War and they were scary for me to look at.

I remember Aunt Cindy making me a pink satin dress to wear to the theater. She took me by the hand, showing me off, telling everyone she knew whom I was.

Uncle John once told me this story.

It seems that whenever they were going to have chicken for dinner, Aunt Cindy would clean it and cut it up, and then throw the feet out to the dogs. It was a "waste not, want not" time in our lives.

Well, one time they had gone off shopping for a long period of time. When they came back home there was a terrible sight to see. All their chickens were flopping around in the yard with no feet. While they'd been gone the dogs had gotten hungry, and because the chicken feet were all they were used to eating, they attacked the chickens and just ate their feet.

My brother, Jim, told how he would go to Uncle John's and he wouldn't be able to find him inside the house. He would go out the back door, and yell for him.

Our Uncle John would be up on top of the house, making roof repairs. He had hauled a ninety-pound roll of tarpaper up a ladder, unrolled it, and was tacking it down in place. Now you must understand that Uncle John, himself, only weighed about ninety pounds, soaking wet.

He had also tied a rope around himself, and then around the chimney, in case he slipped off.

He was 90 years old at the time.

By the time Uncle John was 97 he had cancer under his left eye, and my brother Jim was taking him for medical treatments. Jim told us the doctors at the hospital wanted to know what the different kinds of medication were that Uncle John was taking.

They were astonished when he told them, "Alka Seltzer, vitamins, and a little baking soda if I need it bad enough."

He was on no blood pressure or heart medications?

No special diet or any other restrictions?

Uncle John replied, "No disrespect meant, but that stuff will kill you if you start taking it. I always did all right just working hard and taking a vitamin daily."

When he was in the hospital and things didn't go to suit him, he would verbally threaten the nurses with his nephew, Jim. "Just wait till my nephew gets here," he would say.

Uncle John's memory stayed clear as long as he lived. He was one of the nicest people who ever lived, he was kind, laughed a lot, and had a good sense of humor. On his 100th birthday, someone gave him a teddy bear with a dress and hat on it. To be funny, he named it "Cindy" and said it looked just like her.

One day, a real old lady with gray hair showed up at our house. Mother told us she was our Aunt Cindy, father's sister. She had come to stay with us, and we thought that was just fantastic.

One day she decided to make us some candy. We all stood around the kitchen and watched while she pulled taffy to make into sticky candy. When she finished, she cut it into pieces and put it in canning jars to harden.

She told us when it got hard; she would give us a piece of it. From then on, every time I saw her, she had a piece of taffy in her mouth, sucking on it.

One Saturday night, father went out to drink. Mother told us we had better help Aunt Cindy up the stairs so she wouldn't be down there when father got home.

The next day Aunt Cindy left and never came back.

Once, when we were living in Inman, Virginia, our mother needed to go to the store for something. The store was close to the house where we lived. I can't remember any other time she did this. Our ages were like 6, 5 and 3.

(Left to Right front row) Beatrice (Bootsy) James Jr. (Jim), Magdalene Geraldine in the back center

She sat all three of us on the bed next to the window, so we could see out, and told us not to move. She also told us not to let anyone into the house while she was gone. She said she would only be gone a minute. Now, we were raised to listen to our mother, and we did exactly what she told us to do.

While we were sitting there, looking out the window, this man comes walking up the road in front of our house. When he got to our gate, he opened it, and came on into the yard. He came up to the front door, and started knocking on it. When no one came to answer the door, he came over to the window where we were sitting. He asked us,

"Where is your mother?"

We did not answer him; we just sat there and looked at him. He told us he was our father's brother. We still didn't have anything to say to him. We didn't know what our "father's brother" was, at that age. Anyway, he had black hair, very dark eyes, and he didn't look like anyone we knew, surely not our father.

He went over and sat down on the steps of our house. After a while, our mother came walking up the road with a bag of groceries in her arms. When she saw him sitting on the steps, she started laughing out loud.

He said that he told us kids he was their father's brother.

"Those kids still wouldn't let me in the house," he told her.

She said, "Well, they don't know you, and I told them not to let anyone in." This turned out to be our Uncle Sam.

My father had another sister, named Pearl. Her husband, Walter, would start drinking, and Aunt Pearl was afraid of him. She would make him bring her and her children to our house. She would cry, but her girls, Geneva and Zella Mae would be happy to see us. We were all the same ages, about 8-9 years old. They'd put all four of us girls in one bed. It was fun. We'd tell tales we knew strange stories that were told to scare you.

One night, Geneva was telling one, and when she got to the part where you yelled, "BOO!" to scare everyone, the bed collapsed with us. We were all laughing when my father came in to put the bed back together. He told us we'd better get to sleep.

Uncle Walter would still be outside drinking and driving. He'd drive up and down the road in front of the house, and Aunt Pearl would be crying, saying,

"Oh, he is going to kill himself."

My father would say, "Uncle Walter drives his car like he drives his mining motor in the mines."

We'd ask, "How's that?" He would say, "With the throttle wide open," as he laughed.

Geneva told me that when they didn't come to our house, her mother would sometimes take her and leave her with her Grandmother Scott. Geneva lives in California now. I talk to her on the phone.

She told me Doc Blevins was at McRoberts before he came to Jenkins.

We have a great time talking about the out houses and the honey wagon. She also remembers the time that some of the kids pushed one of the honey wagons down a hill and it went up under somebody's house and lodged itself under the house, and they had to move because of it. She remembers the stories we used to tell. She was good at it. She also tells me about my father teaching her to dance. He did love to dance!

Mother took us to visit her Aunt Mandy and Uncle Mayo when we were still young enough to enjoy ourselves. They lived at Millstone, at the head of a holler, and her father still lived there, too. Her two half sisters, Roberta and Louise, were about our ages. One second cousin, Elizabeth, we called Tootsie, showed us around the farm they lived on.

She took us to a creek, where she gave each of us a stick to probe for turtles. We would find them and play with them. Next we'd go to the barn and climb up in the hayloft.

She told us to lie down on our bellies and spit on the horse that was down below. It started kicking up its heels, and I thought it would kick the barn down.

Then we would go down to Roberta's and visit for a while. Our big adventure there was to slip in the back door and steal Fidel's brown sugar. Fidel was our step-grandmother and Roberta's mother.

Uncle Mayo was really nice. He knew we had never seen the way people live on a farm. He showed us how they stored vegetables in a root cellar. He showed us his garden. And, he showed us how they kept their butter and milk in an abandoned mineshaft, where it was real cold. They had a well for water, too.

Besides taking care of his farm, he climbed the mountain and went over to the next town of Seco, and worked in the mines. He was always smiling; always begging us to eat more. Even after I was in my twenties, I still went there to visit, and I enjoyed it as much as I did when I was a child. The greatest thing ever was to sleep in a feather bed.

While we were living in Inman, my mother's brother came to see her. Someone knocked on the back door, and when my mother opened it, there was this tall man, laughing and hollering "Sis!" and she were hollering "Bill!" He said to her, "Sis, I want you to meet my wife. Her name is Verdi."

That is one time I can truly say I saw my mother happy. I can't remember how long they stayed with us.

Aunt Verdi would dance and hold her dress up in front, just above her knees. I would go outside, behind the house, and dance like her. My two younger sisters and I would laugh. We thought it was funny. I learned, years later, that I had learned the "Hoe-down", by making fun of Aunt Verdi. It was while Uncle Bill and Aunt Verdi were there that my father got a job in the coalmines at Dunham, Kentucky, and we moved. That was in the fall of 1930.

Chapter Seven
Father

About my father – to say the least, he was something else. He had courage. He was not afraid of anything. When you got to know him, and learned about how he grew up, you knew where it came from.

He was courteous, a most polite person. He had the nicest manners. People would tell me how nice he was.

Those who knew him when he was young said, "My, oh my, he was good looking." My mother said that when she met him he "turned on the charm" and she fell for it.

He wasn't a big man. What he lacked in height, he made up for in fortitude. He was 5'8" tall, 145 pounds, and had a shoe size of 7 ½. He had sandy-colored hair with a red beard mixed in with black, and dark brown eyes that looked almost black. He also had one whole and one-half gold cap on his two front teeth. They were something to look at back in those days. You'd never forget his smile.

He was born in Keokee, Virginia. We have two dates for his birth date. The first one is March 18, 1900. The second one, on his army record, is March 10, 1898. My mother said he lied about his age so he could get into the army. His army records show that he served on active duty from October 1917 to June of 1919, with the rank of Corporal.

Before he was 10, he started working in the mines. They had young boys called "trappers." They closed the trap doors and picked slate out of the coal. Working in the coalmines was a dirty, grimy job. That black coal dust got into your pores and no amount of washing could ever get it all out. He died of Black Lung from working all his life in the mines.

Today when I hear young men complain about how hard they work, and what their jobs are I think of all the men in this world who have to work in coal mines. They spend half of their lives under the earth, in the dark, in the coal dust, knowing that in the end, it will kill them.

When our father was about 12 his family moved to Pardee, Virginia. They had been there only a couple of years when his father was killed by a train. It was January of 1914. Our mother told us his father was on the railroad track, and the train ran over him because he didn't hear it coming. Jim, my brother, remembers the story. He says, "Grandfather was crossing the tracks with a wagon when the train hit him." Jim gave me a picture of the mining town that shows where the road crosses the tracks, right where he was killed. We have the death certificate; it lists the cause of death, "Struck by railroad train - accident."

Railroad Tracks in Pardee, Virginia.

Then on Christmas Day of that same year, 1914, our father's mother died. Her death certificate lists her death as "Chronic Internal Nephritis," which is an infection of the kidneys and urinary tract. Uncle John's niece, my cousin Fay Estep, told me in 1993, that before grandfather died, grandmother was already sick. She said he would make a holistic medicine out of herbs for her, but after he died no one knew how to make the medicine and that is why she subsequently died.

There were eight children in my father's family. When their mother died, my father was about 15 years old. He was the one who signed her death certificate. He had two younger sisters, Pearl and Ada. They went to live with our Uncle John, who was twenty-three at the time.

My father told this story from his teenage years. He and his brother, Harvey, were out in the coke ovens over by Norton one winter. The coke ovens were where they burned coal in order to get the solid residue they used for fuel. Well, as he told it, he and Harve got inside one of the ovens, after putting cardboard in to lie down on, and went to sleep.

Later, a black man came and threw my father and uncle out into the cold. They waited for him to go to sleep, and then they took bricks and killed him. After he was dead they pulled him out into the cold, went back inside the oven and back to sleep. I used to listen when my father told this story. He bragged about it. I often wondered if he really did such a thing or not, surely he couldn't have been so cold hearted.

On the 14th of April 1917, John Oxford married Cindy. Six months later, in October of that same year, father and his brother, Harvey, enlisted in the Army at Camp Lee, Virginia. While he was in France, he grew up. Sometimes when he got to drinking, he would tell us things that happened to him while he was over there.

He spoke of how it rained, about all the mud in the trenches, and about being gassed with mustard gas by the Germans and the gas staying under his helmet causing him to have sores on his head for years.

I don't know how young he was when he learned to dance, but he was good at it. He would tell us about when he danced in France, in a big ballroom, and people would throw him money, even from the balcony.

We would ask, "Did you pick it up?" "Yes," he would say, "and I put it in my hat."

He could soft shoe; sand dance, buck and wing, Charleston, and he taught us to dance like the Russians (doing the Mazurka). We all started out dancing, by standing on top of his feet.

Both of my parents loved to sing and dance. The first record player we had was a Victrola. I thought that was what it was, not the brand name of it. I didn't know it was the trademark for that brand of phonograph. It had a handle on the side. You had to crank it up, and had to change the needles all the time.

Before our mother got sick, he laughed and sang a lot. I have pictures of him when he was in WWII. I look at them today, and I think he really was nice looking. But mostly, I remember he was my father, and while I was growing up in the house with him, it was war.

He took pleasure in the razor strap.

If you didn't walk the line, it was always a threat. Sometimes it was his belt. He would start to unbuckle it, and we would straighten right up. We knew he meant it. He never did whip any of us that I can remember.

He had songs he would sing from the war, too. "Yankee Doodle," "Over There," and his favorite "We Are Going to Hang Old Kaiser Bill from the Sour Apple Tree" to the tune of "Glory, Glory Hallelujah." Sometimes, because he had learned some French, he would sing, "When Yankee Doodle learns to parlez vous Francais." Then he would want to know, "Can you parlez vous Francais?" (Can you speak French?) Anyway, he had fun with us.

He had brought a postcard back with him that had a naked lady on it. Our mother would say, "That woman is lying on an animal skin with its tail pulled up between her legs." My father would get red-faced and laugh. They should see what is on TV, now.

He could play the guitar and sing. He knew all the songs of the twenties and then some. I think he knew every song that had ever been written, that he liked, that is. He played the organ, and the harmonica, too.

He tried to teach me to play the guitar, but I never did get any good at it, through no fault of his. I can't remember when we didn't have music and dancing in our home. My father and mother would dance, waltz and fox trot.

We kids would want to, too, and they'd pick the little ones up and dance with them. Then us bigger ones would want to be picked up and dance on his feet. He was always telling us we were "too big."

Once, we went to a Christmas party that had a band from Appalachia. Father showed everyone how I could dance by having me dance with him. Later during the night, he came and woke me up. He had a big smile on his face.

He said he had something Santa Claus had left for me. He gave me a doll with big blue eyes, and put it in the bed with me.

I remember how cold its face was.

Then there was the night they got all dressed up to go to a dance. My mother wore sky-blue chiffon, sheer silk long evening gown with white puffy sleeves. She looked beautiful.

All us kids hung around, watching her get ready. When they returned home, they told us they had won the cakewalk. That's where they put a mark on the floor, play music, and when the music stops, whoever is on the mark gets the cake.

We all hollered, "Where's the cake?"

They said, "We ate it at the dance!"

There was a family of Italians that lived next door to us. We were forbidden speak to them, but my mother could sell them moonshine. They had a party one night and invited my father. We couldn't understand why we couldn't speak to them (which we did when he wasn't around), but he could go over there to party.

Anyway, the night of the party, we went over and climbed on the porch of their house and looked in the windows. One man was playing a saxophone;

another was playing the accordion, and another a mandolin. In the middle of all this was my father, dancing like we had never seen before, with a pretty black-haired lady wearing a navy blue silk dress.

He was swaying and dipping. They would stand side by side, running across the floor doing wild steps. "Oh, God, let's go tell mother what he is doing with that woman," we said.

We ran home, and told her what we had seen, adding, "And, mother, he was holding his cheek next to hers and leaning way over." Our mother calmed us down. "It's all right," she said, laughing.

"She's a friend of ours and just wanted to dance with your father. They're doing the Camel Walk dance." When father came home she told him about it and they both laughed and laughed.

Chapter Eight
Mother

My mother has been dead for 61 years now. She passed away in August of 1944, when I was only 21 years old and my son, Chuck, was only 9 months old. I still can't think of her without pain and sadness. She had a life that was pitiful, for a person who was so beautiful and nice.

Her mother died when she was just a child. There were two other children, Calvin and William "Bill" Tolliver, her brothers. Her father took her to his sister, Mandy's, and left her. She grew up there.

I never did hear her talk about going to school. She would talk about working, and she must have been treated well, and learned a lot, for she knew a lot of things and loved her Aunt Mandy and Uncle Mayo dearly.

James R. Oxford Sr. and Priselander Ida Tolliver taken on their wedding day

When she was in her teens, she went to work in a boarding house in Millstone, Kentucky, for John and Cindy Oxford.

They would become her brother and sister-in-law, and my Aunt and Uncle. She met and married James Ray Oxford Sr. in 1922, at the age of 17.

They moved to Greasy Creek, Kentucky, where I was born in 1923, when she was 18. My mother had six children, five girls and one boy.

She worked hard, taking care of us; she was clean, kept her home and children clean. She could cook and bake anything you ever wanted. She gardened, and canned fruits and vegetables.

She could sing the old songs that we learned later to love; she could also play the organ and banjo. She knew things about how to take care of us with what she called, "old time medicine" we now refer to it as holistic medicine.

I can remember when I was about seven years old, it was night and it was raining, and my mother tied a handkerchief on her head to go out into the dark, rainy night. I was upset at the idea.

She told me, "I have to go down by the creek and get some catnip."

My brother, Jim, was the baby at that time, and had the croup. I know catnip was used to make tea, one of those "old-time" remedies.

She knew all about those kind of things.

Two other medicines we used a lot were Castor Oil and Vicks salve. The Castor Oil was put in orange juice and for me sometimes, even in buttermilk. I used to get boils on my arms. She would wilt beet leaves or get a thin slice of pork and tie them on my arms. This was supposed to bring the boil to a head. Lots of times, when it was all done, it would take a long while for the boil to heal.

When I was about seven, mother was still washing clothes on a washboard in a galvanized tub. My father had me standing between his legs. He told me to call my mother some kind of a bad name, which one I can't remember, for good reason.

She told me, "You better not."

I thought I was safe, with my father there, and I thought the name was funny, so I did.

She told me, "When your father goes to work I will whip you," and she did. It's the only whipping she ever gave me.

I know they moved to McRoberts, where two of my sisters were born. Then they moved to Inman, Virginia, where my brother was born. I can remember they were happy there.

By 1942 our mother had been sick and bedridden for six or seven years. She ran the house from her bed. If she wanted something done and we didn't cooperate with her, all she had to say was, "I will tell your father when he comes home."

We'd make biscuits every morning. We had this pan we baked them in. It must have been made of tin. It's the only kind of baking tin that I have ever used that rusted.

Her final word to us every morning was, "You girls had better wipe that pan before you make those biscuits."

First thing she would do when we took her breakfast was to turn over the biscuits to see if there was any rust on the bottoms. If there was, she peeled the bottom part off and said,

"I thought I told you to wipe that pan."

We'd answer, "We did," knowing full well that we didn't.

Years later I asked her how she knew. She said, "When you put the pan on the hot stove and wiped it, it made a crackling and popping sound." She'd listen for that, and when she didn't hear it, she knew.

She had crippling rheumatoid arthritis. It started when Gloria Ann (Cat) was about a year old, in 1935. She went to Little Rock, Arkansas to a special hospital for treatments in the hot baths, there. She was gone almost a year. We were 12, 11, 9, 6, 4 and 1 then. This may seem unreal to people nowadays, but we children cooked, took care of the house and the baby.

The laundry was sent out, the flat things washed, and we ironed the clothes. I remember the baby crying in the night. Magdalene, my sister, and I would lie in the bed with her on our stomach, taking turns rocking the bed up and down until she would go to sleep.

That Christmas there was no white cake with red cinnamon candy drops on it (mother's specialty). Instead, father gave Magdalene and I some money to buy Christmas gifts for the three small ones. We got a scooter for Jim and two dolls, one for each of our little sisters. We also bought some fruit and nuts. I can remember the oranges; because Christmas was the only time we ever had them

We couldn't have a housekeeper because my father drank liquor and no one would stay with us. He ran true to form even while our mother was gone. He still went off on Saturday nights to get drunk and play cards. Once he brought a woman home with him. We slipped upstairs and saw her in bed with him. I went down to the boarding house, where a policeman named Forie lived.

I told him, "My mother is in the hospital in Arkansas and my father has a woman in the house." He said, "You go home and don't let your father know you've been here."

When I got home, the woman and my father were awake. He told us to fix her some breakfast and coffee.

We had a pantry in the kitchen. In it was a can of lye. Bootsy was for putting lye in her coffee, but Magdalene and I wouldn't let her.

Then the policeman came. Father told him the woman was his housekeeper. All the time he kept looking at me to see if he could tell if I was the one who went and got the cop.

Forie told the woman, "I'm sending a cab for you. Get in it." Then he told father, "And, Mr. Oxford, I don't want to hear that you have whipped any one of these children."

Now you'd think that was enough, but no, he still got drunk. He even sold our mother's sewing machine to pay a fine to get out of jail. It was a great disappointment to my mother when she came home.

Another disappointment was for her to find we had moved while she was gone. The house we had been living in had three bedrooms, clothes' closets, a large kitchen and living room, a big yard and garden.

The house we moved to was Ethel Mullin's house. It had only two bedrooms and running water. She convinced father it would be easier for us to take care of, and she would move into our house. There were no closets, no pantry in the kitchen, small rooms and a small yard. We put mother's bed in the living room because there wasn't any room for it anywhere else. I figure we lived in that house three or four years.

But the saddest thing that happened when mother came home from the hospital was when she called for her baby Gloria Ann and Cat answered, "You are not my mama. My mama's in Hot Springs."

After mother came home, we got a housekeeper, named Ruby. Father put the make on her right away. Mother saw him in the kitchen, pushing Ruby up against the sink. Mother cried and told me about it.

That night, since Ruby and I shared the same bed, I said to her, "You pack your clothes and leave in the morning. And, you'd better not say anything about this to my father, or I will tell your mother what you have been doing with my father." After that night I stayed home from school to take care of my mother. I never did return to finish my education.

Mother finally got her bed moved into one of the bedrooms, put us girls in the other bedroom, and bought a couch that made into a bed for Jim.

When a girlfriend of mine moved to Oak Ridge, Tennessee, her house became empty, and we wanted to move to it. It was like the one Ethel Mullins had cheated us out of. We knew what she had done to our mother, and as we grew older we wouldn't speak to her.

Anyway now the problem was how to move our bedfast mother to the new house. Things had become worse for her. Father had reached across her bed one night to hit one of us children, and he fell on top of mother, breaking her leg just above the ankle. It never did mend right because her bones were soft, from her being sick and bedridden so long. She spent the rest of her life with her foot on a pillow, turned up, with the bone sticking out of her leg. So how do we move our mother? She solved the problem herself. She called the ambulance and they moved her for us.

Father still continued his drinking, but by then we had gotten up enough nerve to go next door to use the phone to call the police. Our neighbor pleaded with us, "Please don't ever let him know you whose phone you are using."

Time and time again he would hit mother, and I would run next door and call the police. The younger kids would tell him, "Geraldine has gone to call the police on you."

He would get up and go into the woods to hide. When the police came, they would call to him. He'd tell the officer that he hadn't done anything. Finally I told them they'd better take him away, because as soon as they left he would start up again.

And, they did. They took him to Jenkins.

The next morning I went to Jenkins with the intentions of making them do something about him and his abusiveness. I met him coming out of the Jenkins Courthouse. He told me he had taken a dry oath. I had to ask what that was.

He said, "If I drink anymore, I will have to do time in jail." I started for the cabstand. He started off in another direction. I told him, "If you don't come home with me, I'm going back into the police station and tell them you were going over to Pound, Virginia to get drunk again."

He laughed and thought that was funny. When we got home, he told my mother,

"Geraldine is going to send me up the river."

After that he complained to mother about not being able to have a drink on account of "those kids of yours." He did slip off and drink, but he didn't come home and start any more fights.

Mother lived until August of 1944. She died at the age of 39. Dora Morefield had come to see her and she told me my mother was dying. I remember telling her, "Oh, mother has been real sick before this and always gotten all right."

It had been raining all that week. It was cold and damp outside. Mother had pneumonia and a fever, and would not take her medicine. I still continued to think that she would get better. I couldn't believe anyone could die that young. She died that same night.

Our father never did put a grave marker on mother's grave. Jim, who was fifteen years old, bought a beautiful marker for her grave some years later.

It was inscribed

Mother

"To Love Is Still To Have"

I have gone back to visit her grave every chance I could.

Chapter Nine
The Scrappers

When I was in the first grade of school, I attended the morning session. There was a boy, also in the first grade that attended in the afternoon session. He would be coming to school when I'd be going home. He would wait to hit me, and would watch me cry. I didn't know why he was hitting me.

Everyday it got worse, from just hitting me to eventually beating on me. I would go home, crying, my mother and father would listen while I would tell them about this boy. I was afraid of him, and I didn't know anything about fighting.

One day on the way home, I decided to go over on the other side of the railroad tracks to get away from him. He laughed at me when he saw what I was doing, and came over to where I was and hit on me again. I went home crying. My mother and father started yelling at me. They told me if I didn't hit him back they would give me a good whipping when I got home.

It was in the winter, with snow on the ground. After school the next day, I started home. Where we walked, the sidewalks were made of wood and up along the side of the hillside, away from the road. Knowing this kid was going to beat me up, and then when I got home my mother and father were going to whip me, too. That was going to be three whippings in one day.

I met him at the coal tipple. It was built across the road and over the railroad tracks. I had made up my mind to fight back. The threat of two whippings when I got home was all the encouragement I needed to become brave.

He came up and hit me in the face; I closed up my fist, and hit him back in the face.

The look of surprise was all I needed, so I started beating up on him. He started hollering and crying. By then I had him on the ground and we rolled about five feet down the bank to the road.

Some men, working in the tipple, came down and pulled me off of him. They told my father they thought I was going to kill him, and they believed if they hadn't stopped me, I would have. After it was over he went on to school, crying. I was muddy from one end to the other, but I went home happy. My mother and father were very proud of me. They both had big smiles on their faces.

A few days later, a man stopped to talk to my father. It was his son I had beat up. He told my father it was his fault, because he had been teasing his son about "that little Oxford girl" being his "sweetheart," and his son had taken it out on me.

When we were small, and our father found our mother out of the house, he'd get my two sisters together and bet them that they could whip me. We would go at it. When it got too rough he would make us stop. All the time he was laughing.

One day when another man was visiting us, my father started it up. "I bet you two girls can't whip her," he said to my sisters, and then pointed towards me. We were fighting pretty strongly when my mother walked in.

She started yelling for us to stop. She told my father, "You should be ashamed, putting your girls up to fighting like that." She told us if she ever caught us fighting again, she would whip us.

What my mother didn't know was, he was actually doing us a favor. There were times after that, at school, and other places when it came in handy. When push came to shove, the other kids soon learned to leave us alone because they knew we all could fight. We earned the reputation of being "The Oxford Girls".

I remember one time at the milk gap. That's where everyone went to milk the cows. Sometimes we would go up there to watch the cows and the women milking them. Rita Mullins' mother's cow had a calf. I put my hand through the fence to pet it and Rita picked up a stick. She came over and was going to hit me for petting the calf. I saw her coming.

She was a head taller than I was at the time.

What she didn't know was that I wasn't going to let her hit me with the stick. I jerked it out of her hand and beat her with it till she started running for home.

She told her mother she got hit for no reason.

When her mother found out the full story, she gave Rita a whipping.

Things happened to all four of us girls, as we grew up and after we were grown, that makes me believe those fights our father put us up to helped to make survivors, or "scrappers", out of all of us.

Our father was the original "scrapper".

Lots of things happened to him in his life that brought it out. At about the same time as he was teaching us to fight, he took the whole family, on a drive to Virginia one day. We had been gone all day and it was starting to get dark. While driving back home, through a part of the Virginia countryside called Pound; we drove past a Roadhouse. (Today they are called bars.)

Standing outside were some men who had been drinking. One of them shined a spotlight into our car and right in my father's eyes. It made father angry, but he kept right on driving all the way home. As soon as we were there and out of the car, he turned around to go back to Pound, all the while our mother begging him not to go. I remember asking my mother why he was so mad.

She said, "They could have caused your father to wreck the car and kill us all."

The next morning when we got up, we knew something had happened. There was not a place on his face or hands that didn't have a scratch or cut on it. We drew pictures of him with scratches all over his face. He thought they were funny and laughed.

He had gone back to Pound and gotten into a fight with those same men. He told us that the fight was so bad they ended up in Jenkins Hospital. While the doctor was fixing his cuts and scratches he felt something in his mouth, over on the side where the jawbone was. He put his finger in to feel what it was and pulled out the end of someone's finger.

He must have bitten it off in the fight. I wonder if he did what Mike Tyson said he did

"Lost it in the heat of the fight."

There were three men he got into the fight with. Two were from Hammond, and the other man was Pat Perkins, Lawrence Perkins' father. Pat lived in Strait Row, where we lived. Whenever he went anywhere he had to pass our house. His face was scratched up just like our fathers. After that, whenever he'd go past our house he would look the other way.

He was embarrassed for his part in it.

I think we had gotten ourselves a little reputation. Because, sometime after that, we needed a hog slaughtered. My mother hired one of the Blevins' boys to do it. Evidently, he had some trouble with trying to get it out of the pen.

I came into her room one day and she was laughing. I asked her what was so funny.

She said the Blevins' boy had told her,

"That God-dang hog was just like those Oxford kids were meaner than hell."

I wanted to know why he said that. She said, "I guess it tried to bite him while he was trying to get it out of the pen."

Chapter Ten
The "Moonshine" Years

One September day, mother went into labor and we called Dr. Stanfield. He came and examined my mother and told her it would be sometime before the baby would be born.

She told him, "Doc you are wrong."

When he got back to his office, there was a message waiting for him. It told him that my sister had been born, and to get back to our house right away.

Our mother decided to keep a couple of boarders. There were the two brothers, Frank and Herman Carter that moved into our house. One of them, Frank, was married, and his son came to stay over the weekends with his father. The other one, Herman, got married and moved out.

My mother bought herself a sewing machine with the money from the boarders. She made clothes for all of us. I remember her making all three of us girls' dresses alike, which we were happy to have. She even made little suits for our brother, Jim.

After the boarders were gone, my mother and father started making "home brew," which I later learned was beer. I watched them make it enough that I think I could have made it by myself.

They would bottle it up and put it in mason quart jars.

Under our house there was a spring and the water was ice-cold. They would take the jars down there and bury them in the sand under the spring water.

Once when I was about eight or nine, I went down there and decided to drink one of them, not really knowing what it was that I'd be drinking. I came out from under the house, went into the kitchen where my mother was and sat down on a chair. It felt like my chair or the floor was moving.

My mother took one look at me and said,

"Have you been under the house drinking that beer?" I don't remember anything after that. I know I never did drink any more of it. She and my father said they'd whip me if I did.

At the same time, they were selling moonshine by the pint. My mother would get ready to go to the store. She'd set all the pints of liquor up on the drain board at the sink, and tell me,

"You are not to go out of the house. You are to watch the window, and if Doc Blevins comes up the road, you are to pour this down the drain."

I'd ask, "What do you want me to do that for?" She made me understand that he was the Sheriff, and if he found the moonshine in the house, she'd go to jail.

In Dunham, KY, there was a small store that Consolidated Coal Company built. It even had a scrip office and a meat counter. When I think back, I must have been about 10 or 12 when this happened.

I was in the store when they had gotten some fish in. The manager's name was Vivian, and he was going on about this big old fish they had gotten, and it was BIG. I went home and told my mother about it.

She handed me a heavy oatmeal box, telling me to take it back to the store, give it to Vivian, and tell him that she wanted that fish. When I gave him the box, he took it into the back of the store.

He came back with a smile, wrapped up the fish, and told me to tell my mother,

""Thank you."

Oh yes, I forgot to say that a quart of moonshine was in the oatmeal box, and I thought he was crazy for taking oatmeal for a BIG fish.

Our lives were a "living hell" from 1931 to 1935. I have gone back and put together our ages and what happened, and come up with this. My father (James Ray Oxford Sr.) started beating our mother whenever he got drunk. She had my younger sister in 1931. That was when it started, and it lasted until 1935. I can't remember that he hit her before then, when she was pregnant, but after Gloria Ann (Cat) was born, in 1934, she couldn't walk right. She dragged her foot, and used a stick to help herself along.

During those years, he would get drunk and start beating mother. We would hear her crying, and we would run out of the house, screaming and crying into the night. Our neighbors would hear us, and look out their doors; some would come out and just stand on their porches.

Sometimes, during the winter, we would be standing out there in the snow. We always seemed to be barefoot, and in our slips. That's what we slept in, our slips. That would be the only thing we had on, besides our panties. Our father would come out and try to get us to come back into the house.

He would tell us, "I'm going to whip you if you don't come in!" But, we still wouldn't go back inside the house. Finally, our mother would come outside, into the cold, and tell us he had gone to bed and that it was safe for us to come in and go to bed now.

Once, during the night, our father kicked our mother, in the small, bottom part of her lower back, near her tailbone. After that she had a big knot there and it hurt her the rest of her life.

My brother, Jim, told me he could remember seeing our mother on the floor, and our father beating her. He was only 4-6 years old when this happened.

The worst of the drunken incidents, for us children, was one I will never forget.

One night, after he came home, he came into our bedroom and turned the light on to wake us all. Our mother had two beds in this room. I was in the bed across from the one Jim slept in. Jim was somewhere around 4 years old, and I was around 10. The light fixture in this room was just an electric cord, with the light bulb hanging on the end of it.

There was a switch to turn it on and off. Our father went over and sat on Jim's bed. He had a gun in his hands. He was pointing the gun at the light bulb and betting Jim that he could shoot it out.

Jim just shook his head up and down, agreeing with what ever our father said. I had pulled the covers up over my head, and was pretending to be asleep. I heard the shot ring out, the glass shattering on the floor, and when I peeked out of one corner of the blanket, all I could see was the darkness.

We were all terrorized and screaming.

Our mother ran into the room shouting, "What have you done?"

Our father just laughed.

Chapter Eleven
The Coal Mines

In his early years, father was a brakeman. His job was to run and switch cars to different tracks where they were needed to be loaded with coal. I use to watch my father getting ready to go to work. After he was dressed he would take friction tape, and starting just below his knees he would wrap it all the way down to his ankles so his pants would not get caught on the cars and get ripped. Then he would wrap it around his shoes, trying to make them last longer. He wore a carbide lamp on his cap, and carried a lunch pail. The lunch pail had water in the bottom and a place for food in the top. He would always bring something back for the "baby" in the family, who would run out to get his lunch pail when he got home.

For years his job was to hand load coal into coal cars. The number of cars he loaded paid him. To keep track of how many cars he did each day; he had to have "checks". Checks were about the size of a dollar and had numbers on them. They also had holes in them so they could be carried on a piece of wire. When the car was fully loaded, he just pulled a "check" off the wire and hung it on the coal car.

Some miners, who worked in the lowest parts of the mine, had to wear something that looked like the sole of a shoe on one knee. Some also had to strap a piece of leather to their back to keep the sharp edges of the coal from cutting their backs while they crawled along in the mine.

When we lived in Inman, VA, the coalmine shut down and he was without work. He went with some other men to Dunham, KY, to get work. He had to leave us behind. My mother was crying. Then we started crying. He told us he'd whip us if we didn't shut up.

My mother said, "Oh, no you will not!" And, he didn't. All of this was going on during the great depression years. I can still hear him telling my mother, "It's Hoover's fault," because he said, "that all a man needed was a dollar a day and a pair of overalls."

I know working conditions got better for him at Dunham. There, he ran a cutting machine. It cut the coal, and they had machines to do the loading. Where they use to using a lot of timber to hold up the tops, now they used steel pins. They also had battery lights on their hats. His lunch box had a thermos bottle, and mother had us make him ham sandwiches and put in a piece of fruit for dessert. He was paid by the hour, and in 1936, the miners went on strike to help John L. Lewis form a union for the coalminers over in Harlan.

During the strike, some of the men wanted to keep working. They were called "scabs".

The strikers, who wanted the union, wouldn't let the workers pass the lines. The Coal Company called in the National Guard to help the "scabs" get to work safely. The Guard had machine guns, there were many people killed, cars were dynamited, tear gas was used, and most of the miners' daughters were dating men in the Guard.

Father and his friend, C. L. Martin, went to Harlan often. My mother worried about him, as he would come home, telling about turning over cars. The strike caused Harlan to have a bad name.

They called it "Bloody Harlan" for many years to come.

While they were out on strike, we ate soup beans every day. Mother cooked beans we had never seen before, like cranberry beans. We hated them! All three of us girls would sing, "Beans, beans, the musical fruit. The more you eat, the more you toot!"

Mother would try to get us to stop, but we would just laugh.

Every weekend father would get cleaned up to go to town, gambling and drinking with the other miners. His pants were sent out to the cleaners and his dress shirts to the laundry. When he went out on the weekends, he wore a suit and tie, and his shoes were shined.

Oh, and let's not forget his hat! He used to entertain us kids with his hat. He knew how to make us believe he threw money through it.

He took great pride in his appearance.

James Ray Oxford, Sr.
Born March 10, 1898 in Keokee, Virginia
Died February 18, 1968

Chapter Twelve
The "White Castle" Kid

My brother, Jim, sold hamburgers at the entrance to the mines when the night shift came to work. He started selling them when he was twelve, and sold them until he was fifteen. One of us girls would fry them for him. He put them together with mustard, onions and pickles. We would wrap them in waxed paper, and put them in a container. We would make fifty hamburgers, and the one that fried them got one to eat.

He sold the hamburgers for 10 cents each. I still have to believe that he was the original White Castle Kid, because the buns were the size of the White Castle burgers.

He took coffee, and sold it for 5 cents a cup.

Jim used that money to buy all his clothes and a bike. He would be at the mines sometimes real late at night, and he would fall asleep. The miners would take their burgers and coffee, leaving the money for him without waking him up.

Honesty was never an issue back in those days.

One night we had a big snow in the mountains. The miners who lived in Virginia couldn't get home, and they were hungry. Jim came home and tried to find what he could to take back something they could eat. They told him they didn't care what it was, even a pot of beans would do, and that they would pay for whatever he could find.

He made sure they had a hot meal, and they did pay him for it, with money and appreciation.

Chapter Thirteen
Segregation

The children of Jenkins were raised during the age of segregation. To seg-re-gate meant to impose the separation of a race or class, and in those days, which was the norm, the standard, model, or pattern regarded as typical for a specific group.

When the Consolidated Coal Company came to Jenkins to open up the mines, and build towns, segregation is what they imposed. They built schools for the white children and schools for the colored children.

Everything they built, the stores and recreation halls, were segregated. A Greek man, named Jimmy, was manager of the colored recreation hall. There were stores just for the colored people also.

One of the white recreation halls had a theater in it. The colored people could go upstairs to sit in the balcony, but I can't remember ever seeing anyone up there. The theater showed silent movies most of the time and cowboy movies with sound, sometimes.

I can remember seeing "Drums along the Mohawk" there. My brother, Jim, told me that he and some of his friends had found a way to get into the upstairs of the theater by climbing through a window.

When they did that, they got to see the movies for free.

The stores they built were General Stores, where you could buy any and all kinds of merchandise. I would say they were the first "Sams" and "Big Lots" types of general stores. There was one thing better – you could go there, draw out what was called "Company Money" (script), and spend it without ever having to leave the store.

In the same store was the town Post Office. There were two windows to get mail from, and over each window was a sign. One said "Colored" and the other one, "White".

They built houses in "hollers", all over the hillsides, and gave these places names. Each place had a grade school and a small company store, where you could get groceries.

When the children got out of grade school, they rode the bus to Jenkins to attend high school. They built a school for the colored children that went up to the twelfth grade, over in a town called Dunham.

The white and colored men didn't work together in the coalmines. They each worked in different sections of the mines. You could see them going to work, from where we lived on Barn Hill. They rode in separate mining cars called the "man trip". The white men were the only ones allowed the use of the bathhouse. The colored men had to bathe at home.

Chapter Fourteen
Third Grade

When I was in the third grade, the teacher knew that I was hard of hearing; something the diphtheria had left behind. The teachers that I had for first and second grade made me sit up front so I could hear the lessons. In the third grade I was sat almost in the back of the classroom.

Geraldine (second from the left)
School Picture

They had a Christmas play in which I was to read "The Night before Christmas." I can remember I wanted to *say* it and the teacher wanted me to *read* it.

I had memorized the entire story.

My teacher complained to my mother that she couldn't make me understand what she wanted me to do.

My mother's answer was, "She has memorized it, let her say it."

Mrs. White wasn't too happy with that.

We had a visiting health nurse come to our school. She weighed about 200 pounds, was six feet tall, with short dark hair, glasses, and wore a blue uniform. Between Mrs. White and this nurse they convinced my mother that I needed to be sent to Danville, KY, to the school for "deaf and dumb" children because I couldn't hear well. My mother made me some new dresses. I was happy about getting the new clothes, and getting to ride on the train.

It was a great place. They taught everything there. They taught the girls to cook and the boys to be tailors. Mr. Lee, who was in charge, took us all over the place. We ate in a large dining room.

Then he took us to the music room. There was a baby grand piano with about ten children standing around it, singing "springtime in the Rockies." They sounded funny to me, but then I didn't know that they were deaf.

Mr. Lee gave us a room to sleep in for the night. The next day he took my mother and I to a classroom. He had me face the blackboard and asked me to write my name. I kept turning around to see what he was saying.

He explained that he didn't want me to turn around; he wanted to find out how well I could hear. I wrote my name. Then he asked me to write where I lived, and I did. After that he got angry and started talking to my mother about my hearing loss not being that bad.

He wrote two letters, one to the nurse telling her to mind her own business and take care of the sick children; and another one to the principal telling him to make the teachers do their jobs. Telling us that I didn't belong at Danville, my mother got ready to leave. I wanted to stay; I thought it was very interesting and quite a unique place.

She said, "You don't belong here and we are going home."

She took great pleasure in giving those letters to the nurse, the principal, and telling everyone about our trip and the school.

School was the same for me. I would just sit where I wanted. They never did make me sit up front; they treated me just like the rest of the kids. I don't think they cared if we learned or not.

I remember the music teacher was from Paris, KY. Her name was Miss Allison. She would go from room to room teaching music. If any of the kids acted up in class, she would run down the aisle and grab their hair and pull it. The kids didn't tell on her because the code was, if you get a whipping in school you're sure to get one at home, too.

But, one finally did. Her mother came to school and told the principal what she was going to do to Miss Allison. The principal took her into his office and sent for the teacher. The mother was talking, Miss Allison was crying, and all of us kids thought it was funny. She never did pull anyone's hair again. My mother said she'd better never pull any of her children's hair.

There were a lot of smart kids in my class, and I knew it.

I would ask my mother, "How did they get so smart?"

Her answer was, "Their fathers were store managers and knew how to help them."

One of the kids was real smart. His father was a foreman in the mines. I was too young to understand then, but I know now my mother was telling me that the parents of these kids were well educated.

Chapter Fifteen
Nostalgia

Sometimes I get nostalgic remembering my life in the mountains. In 1987 when my daughter, Sharon, was helping me wallpaper and stencil my house in Missouri, she taught me this new word. The wallpaper I liked looked real old and had flowers and roses on it.

She said, "Mother, we are nostalgic about the things we like."

I looked it up in the dictionary to see what it meant. It means "a longing for things, persons, or situations that are not present, home sickness, a return to yesterday".

My memories of living in a Coal Company town are many. The Company took care of everything. They even paid for our family's medical care. If we got sick when the Doctor had office hours, we just went and waited our turn. You didn't have to wait long; there were never that many people sick. If you needed to go to the hospital, the doctor sent you. That was all paid for, too. But if you had to go to the dentist, you paid for that yourself.

When you went to the doctor's, there was always someone there you knew, and you'd sit and talk until one of you were called to see the doctor. If you got sick with any kind of contagious disease, you were quarantined for thirty days. They would nail a sign on your house to let everyone know. The only person who could go out of the house was the father, to work.

Most of the women had their babies at home. If it was in the summer, and the windows were open. You knew just how hard a labor they were having by how much screaming you could hear.

My mother told us that babies were what the doctor brought in that little black bag he carried. When we asked about the sore on the babies' bellies, I remember being told that it was caused by a big hook on the end of a big, long stick used to get the babies out of a big pond they were swimming in.

We had an iceman that delivered ice to our homes. The way you let him know that you needed ice was to put the sign out. The sign was diamond-shaped and had four weights, 5, 10, 25, and 40. You'd put the weight you wanted on the top, and he'd leave a block in just that size.

There were coalhouses to store your coal in. The coal was dumped into an opening at the top, and you got your coal out at the bottom. Just because our father worked in the mine, however, didn't mean we got a break on the price of coal. We paid just the same as outsiders did.

It was mostly the children's job to chop wood and carry the coal in to be used in the stoves. The older ones got up in the morning, started the fires in the stoves and fireplaces. You could always tell who was up, by the smoke coming out of the chimney.

A lot of people in that part of the country still use coal in their homes. In the valleys you can see the smoke rising up. It is a peaceful scene. A warm fire in the stove, and a breakfast made up of biscuits and gravy, fried apples, peaches we had canned in the summer, fresh eggs from the chickens we raised, and pork from the hog we butchered.

Mother made all of us work during the summer putting fruit and vegetables up for the winter. Father would dig a root cellar into the side of the mountain on Barn Hill, and built shelves in it. On the shelves we put all the stuff we canned.

One year I remember counting seven hundred half-gallon jars. On the floor, which was bare earth, we had ceramic crocks full of sauerkraut and mixed pickles. Mixed Pickles is a southern dish. It has corn, green beans, cabbage and onions all mixed together and put in pickling brine. We still make it to this day, although it is a lot more work now.

Nature took care of the temperature in the root cellar. It was cool in the summer and warm enough in the winter not to freeze. Father also built a smokehouse. When we killed a hog, the meat was stored in it.

Another thing we did was to string up green beans to dry. In the winter we would soak them in water and then cook them with a piece of salt pork.

When the beans were dried like this, they were called, "shucky beans".

They have their own taste, and even people who had never eaten them before, liked them. One year we even made hominy, which took one whole day. It is really strange when your mother tells you to put lye in the water, and you know lye is a poison.

She had a lot of explaining to do on that day.

Mother would pick blackberries in the summer and can them. When she'd get ready to go pick berries, she'd wear a long-sleeved shirt to cover her arms, so the thorns wouldn't scratch her, and tie her hair up in a handkerchief. Then she'd get a stick to carry to beat the bushes first.

That way, if there were any snakes, they would leave before she started picking.

Our neighbor ladies would ask her, "Aren't you afraid of getting snakebites?"

She'd say, "No, this is why I carry a stick to run them off with."

When winter came she'd make blackberry cobbler for us, which was yummy! We would eat it while it was still hot, and pour a little milk on it.

Yes, I am nostalgic when I relive memories and go back to the mountains. I wouldn't want to live there now, because it isn't the same. But I still get that feeling of how it was, when I was young, and this brings comfort.

Chapter Sixteen
The Honey Wagon

In Jenkins there was a part of town that was set aside for housing the people that the Company brought in. The Executives and Professional people, doctors, nurses, and teachers, store managers and mining engineers. This section was called Lakeside.

There, they built a clubhouse and had extremely nice homes. You had to be somebody to live there. The houses they built for the miners were good; some even had fireplaces, hardwood floors and plastered walls. Most of them had running water; some even had bathrooms. A lot of them had outside toilets. At Halloween, we thought it was a big joke to push them over.

In those days, waste was hauled away by a big old wagon made of steel or iron. It was pulled by at least six big workhorses. On the top was a trap door where the waste went. How they did this was by opening up the back of the outhouse through a slanted trap door, dipping the waste out with a gallon bucket that was attached to a big stick, and emptying the bucket into the wagon's trap door. The "dipper" was known as a honey dipper, and so the children called the wagon, the Honey Wagon.

In Dunham there was a part of town called Strait Row. Quite a few miles outside of Strait Row there is a holler with a couple of very big and wide holes in the ground.

That's where they emptied their Honey Wagon.

I remember we had a black bird dog, named Frank. One day we were up in the holler where the honey holes were.

Frank thought it was a lake of water. He jumped in and started swimming.

You should have heard us kids screaming. When he got out we put him in the creek and washed him off, but mother still gave him a good bath after we got home.

In later years they got a truck for the Honey Wagon. Instead of dipping the waste they stood on top of the truck with hand pumps, and pumped it out of the outhouses.

One of the funny things (funny to us, not to her) that happened around the outhouses was when a girl named Loretta fell in one.

Loretta had red hair and was about ten to twelve years old. Outhouses had front doors you used to go into the outhouse as well as little trap doors on the backside that were used for the waste removal.

We lived on Barn Hill. Our outhouses were not built right behind our houses on Barn Hill, but away from our houses over on another hill. You had to climb steps to get to them.

One day the children were playing up in the hills behind our houses, running up and down the hills. Loretta ran right into the backside of one of the outhouses. It fell and she fell, going right through the little trap door in the back, and into the toilet. She was the butt of jokes for a long time. No pun intended.

Chapter Seventeen
The Thirties

In 1934 my mother had another baby. They named her Gloria Ann. We called her Cat. I begged my mother to name her Kathleen, after a girl I was a friend with. She wouldn't, so I called her Kathleen anyway. I was the one who took care of her.

If anyone asked what her name was, I'd say, "Kathleen."

She was a cute baby. She had blonde, curly hair, and as she got older we'd make "banana curls" out of it.

When she was about three years old, she would get up early in the morning when everyone else was sleeping, and slip out of the house to go across the road to the neighbors, the Vaughan's. Mrs. Vaughan would be up early to get breakfast for her husband. He worked the day shift in the mines, and Cat would go over there to eat breakfast with them. It embarrassed my mother. She would apologize and tell them she'd try to keep her home. They just laughed and said they were happy to have her.

In 1938, when I was fifteen years old, a girlfriend of mine was dating a boy named, Clarence. He had two friends, Dude and Arnold. Well, they fixed it for another girlfriend and I to have dates with them. I got Arnold. I found out his father worked on the Honey Wagon. I didn't want anything to do with him.

They were telling me how nice he was and I shouldn't act the way I was. "Oh, come on, let him kiss you," they said.

Then they got the bright idea to hold me down and let Arnold kiss me. I didn't fight with them, or try to get loose. I just told Arnold,

"If you kiss me, I will kill you when I get loose."

He left and went home, and so did everyone else.

In 1939 we moved into Quiet Row. We were back into a house like we were living in when our mother went into the hospital. It was good to be out of that little house. Now we had one extra bedroom and a clothes' closet.

Everyone was in school, but me. We were teenagers, 16, 15 and 13. We were starting to let boys walk us home from church. They would come to our house and sit on the front porch. Some of the young men had cars.

Our brother, Jim, would come out and tell the boys who our father was, with a big smile on his face, and the boys would just get up and leave.

Chapter Eighteen
Clarence King Morefield Sr.

We were still living in Quiet Row when Clarence came home on leave in 1940. I was seventeen. He came to see me, and we dated while he was home. He looked good in his uniform, a handsome man. He was 6' tall, very athletic, had a nice smile and disposition.

I was flattered that he wanted to date me.

He would come from Jenkins in a cab to pick me up to take me to the movies. We would bring a bag of candy "party mix" along to give to my family. He was nice, and my father and mother really liked him.

Clarence had been in the service for two years at Fort Monroe, Virginia. He was a lifeguard at Virginia Beach, and had some pictures of the girls he knew. I knew he was very worldly, and wanted to teach me.

I was only interested in hugging and kissing, still afraid of doing what "nice girls" didn't do. Because if you did "that" the boy would tell all the other boys, people would talk bad about you, and you might get pregnant. Boys would promise you anything if you would do "that".

I didn't have a clue what "that" was all about?

When Clarence went back to Fort Monroe, we wrote to one another until he came back home. We dated for a few months and then he asked me to marry him. My mother wanted me to be married at home. I had a new blue dress, they got me a wedding cake, and we had pictures taken.

Clarence King Morefield, Sr. and Geraldine Oxford

It was July 19, 1941, and the ceremony was performed in my mother's bedroom so that she could watch me get married. Then we went to his mother's house. We were going to stay with her until we could find us a place of our own.

The first signs of his jealousy showed up within the first couple of months of our marriage, but I didn't know it then. We would go to the movies, and if I saw anyone I knew from Dunham, and spoke with them or smiled at them, he would become angry.

He would jerk me by the arm and say, "Come on." I often wondered what the matter with him was.

When Louise came home from Oak Ridge, Tennessee to visit, he would hardly let me speak to her. My mother told me later how hurt she was. That green-eyed monster was loose back then, and I didn't have the sense to know it.

We lived with his mother and talked about getting a place of our own. Then as the war got worse, we didn't talk about it anymore. We knew he would have to go off and fight.

One late evening, in the fall of 1941, everyone ran outside. The sky was lit up with many colored, flashing lights. No one knew what was going on.

Someone said the flashes were from the war in Europe.

It was a rare thing to see.

I think it was the only time we saw it, the Aurora Borealis lights in the northern sky.

After Franklin D. Roosevelt (FDR) declared war in January of 1942, Clarence left for California. He had already been in the service for three years, and was given the rank of Sergeant. I stayed with his mother awhile and then went back to my parents' house.

Clarence King Morefield Sr.
Born on November 4, 1918 in Rowdy, Virginia
and he died September 16, 1989 in Detroit, Michigan.

Things had changed there. Bootsy and Magdalene had more freedom. They went dancing whenever they could. They had both learned the jitterbug, and they took pleasure in teaching me. They both knew I loved to dance. When they were getting ready to go out, I wanted to go, too.

They told me I couldn't because I was "married." I told them I didn't care I was going anyhow. After all I loved to dance; Clarence was away in the service and would never know, so I was going.

We had a cousin over in Millstone that loved to dance, too, and she had a car. She would come pick us all up, and we would take off to go dancing. Clarence's sister, Catherine, would write and tell him that I had a boyfriend, and I'd have to write and tell him the truth.

(War Rations)

For sugar one pound every two weeks, gas was rationed to 25-30 gallons per week, everything was rationed, meats, and canned goods. In service women were (wave's) in the navy and (wac's) in the army.

Air raids were practiced which were black outs and they were referred to as "air raid drills."

People grew victory gardens, women really started to wear slacks, because of factory work and smocks over their hair. Dresses got short to save material, no silk stockings, silk was for parachutes.

Women used to use leg makeup. After the war ended for a long time there was still a shortage of things, soap and wash powder were among them.

I lived with my in laws, they would not let my father in law have soap for me, I was pregnant and we didn't have a car, I would walk half a mile to the store to get some and walk back.

Chapter Nineteen
California

When Dude, a friend of Clarence's was ready to go back to California, after being home on leave, I decided to go with him to be with my husband. I wanted to go, but my mother was really upset about my going. She ordered me a suitcase from Montgomery Wards anyway, and a cousin gave me a green suit.

I had been getting an allotment, so I already had bought a few clothes. Red has always been my favorite color, so I had a red pantsuit, a red dress, and a red and black dress. I also took a blue pantsuit, a green dress, a yellow sweater, brown and white shoes, a tan-colored coat, and the white rabbit fur jacket that my husband had bought me for Christmas. Mother also gave me twenty dollars, which she made me pin in my bra.

The trip to California took three days and two nights from Kentucky. I can't say that I enjoyed it. The word I can think of to describe how I was is "backwards", and I wouldn't get up out of my seat unless I had too.

I only ate when a vendor came through the train selling food and drink. My feet swelled so bad I didn't dare take my shoes off, and I don't remember ever changing my clothes.

We were on an old coal-burning train from Kentucky to Kansas. The smoke and cinders covered everything, and if you opened the windows, it was all over you. In Kansas we got on the Zephyr, a newer train, which was a lot better.

Many times, during the trip, the conductor would come through and say the train was being sidetracked for a troop train. As it would go by, you could see the tanks and guns on flatbeds. When that happened, everyone would stop talking and just sit and look out the windows.

The feeling you had can't be described, but it was like "overwhelming dread." Now you knew for sure there was a war going on. It was right there in front of you. And young men were going to give their lives to protect us.

Clarence met us at the train stop. I was so tired from the trip that I wasn't even happy to see him. He was happy to see us, though, and then Dude left to go on to San Diego.

A woman, who was expecting a baby, came over to the barracks where the soldiers were staying and asked if one of their wives could come and live with her while she had her baby. That is where I lived for the first few months.

I did enjoy the family I lived with. They had a little girl, and when the baby was born, it turned out to be a little boy. They had this idea that everyone who lived in the mountains had to know how to cook "soul" food and make "moonshine".

I did make fried green tomatoes and cornbread, but that was about it.

After the baby was born, Clarence paid for me to stay with another friend. These people had a little boy, and her husband worked at Douglas Aircraft. Clarence didn't want me to go to work because he knew he was going to be shipped out soon. He would come up on weekends from San Pedro, and we would go places together.

We went to Hollywood to see Louis Armstrong, we went to downtown Los Angeles to Chinatown to eat Egg Fu Yung, and we even went to a burlesque show. I was shocked and embarrassed, but the servicemen were all laughing, including Clarence.

The family I lived with took me to the beaches and to San Bernardino to see the orange groves. When we went to Long Beach, I had the first shrimp I had ever eaten. I loved them then, and still do to this day.

In May of 1943, there was a shortage of lead, and a need for miners to work in the mines. Any serviceman that had mine-working experience could volunteer to go work in the mines in Idaho. Clarence was one of them.

These volunteers were considered "on leave" from the service. You would get paid from the Mining Company, but you were still legally in the service.

I had just found out I was pregnant, and I made plans to go home to Kentucky to have the baby. Clarence went to Idaho. The trip back to Kentucky was just as long as it had been going to California.

When the cab let me out at our house my heart was pounding so hard, I could hardly breathe. Just the sight of the house! The pink roses on the fence were the most beautiful sight I had ever seen. I was home. I didn't realize how much I missed it all until right then.

I had no money because my allotment had stopped coming. Then came a letter from the Government stating that if a wife wanted to be with her husband in Idaho, they would move them out there. Even though my whole family wanted me to stay home, I wanted to be with Clarence when our baby was born. So in September, I left to go to Idaho.

Chapter Twenty
Idaho

Once I left Kentucky, the first place I had to change trains was Cincinnati, Ohio. The station there was impressive. It had a big domed ceiling. Chicago was big, too. The train went through St. Paul, Minnesota, North Dakota and Missoula, Montana. When I took the cab from the train station to the bus stop, the cab driver gave me silver dollars for change.

I told him I didn't want "them."

And he said, "Lady that is all you are going to get out here!"

Clarence met me at the bus station. He was living in a home where the family had room to take in a couple of servicemen. He shared a bedroom with another young man. They all called Clarence "Chuck", and acted real nervous. I didn't know what that was all about, but later I dreamed that Clarence had a girlfriend named Lizzie before I came there. He said there was nothing to it. He had just walked her home and kissed her. He never would believe that I had a dream about it. And I didn't believe his story, either.

I thought we had mountains in Kentucky, but they were nothing like the ones in Idaho. The Rocky Mountains looked they had been stacked one on top of the other. Everywhere in between was a road, or a creek, and in wide places were the towns. The town of Wallace wasn't too big, but it had a place where Clarence could gamble. After he got there, that's all he did. The slot machines were everywhere, even in the gas stations.

While we were there, Clarence got sick with a fever. He wouldn't let me call a doctor, but Grace, the lady that operated the gas station and motel where we were living, finally convinced him to let her call one. We found out he had pneumonia.

At Christmas my mother sent a care package, a box full of things. There was a salt-cured ham, dried shucky beans, food stamps and some gowns she had Magdalene sew on her machine for the baby. I was both pleased and amazed at getting the ham by mail.

Chapter Twenty-One
The Arrival of Chuck

On February 12, 1944, I decided to give myself a perm. I did everything I was supposed to, but left the curlers in when I went to bed. The next morning I awoke in great pain. I had to wake up Clarence to go next door and get the couple who lived there, Mimi and Bill. I was in labor. Mimi took all the curlers out of my hair. I had the curliest head of hair for my trip to the hospital that you have ever seen. Two women friends were in the hospital room with me. They told me to hold on to the top of the bed, and bear down.

Every once in awhile the nurse would come into the room, examine me, and say, "She is not dilating like she is supposed to be."

The hard labor went on for most of the day. They must have given me some kind of drug, because I remember going into the delivery room, and then I lost consciousness.

When I woke up I was back in bed in the hospital room in my bed. When they brought my baby boy to me, there were marks on both sides of his little head, and the nurse said they were from using the forceps. My beautiful little boy weighed eight and one-half pounds and was very long. I named him after his father (as tradition was to be continued with the first-born male child). Since Clarence liked the name Chuck, we called him Chuck.

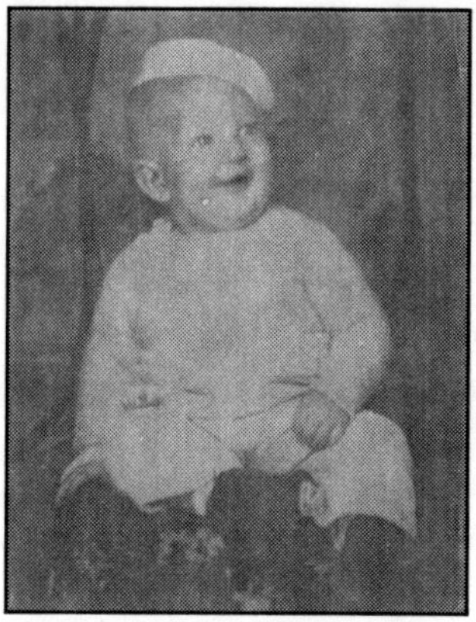

Clarence King Morefield Jr.
Born on the February 13, 1944 in Wallace, Idaho.

There were a lot of babies born that day, and the majority of them were little girls. When I went to the doctor's office for his check-up, there were all those tiny little girls, in their tiny little dresses. Chuck was a big baby, dressed in a long gown. He could hold up his head and look around. I was so very proud of him. The other women couldn't believe he was the same age as their babies.

While I was nursing him, I would go out in the cold air to hang out his clean diapers on the clothesline. I got a cold in my breasts and could no longer nurse him. The doctor gave me something to dry the milk up and I put Chuck on the bottle. Clarence hired a woman that lived nearby, to wash the diapers for me until I got well enough to do it myself.

One day, while bathing, I started crying. I felt so tired; I didn't feel like I was ever going to be my old self again. I know now that I had Postnatal Depression. Clarence would ask me what the matter was. I told him that I didn't know; maybe I was just homesick.

I don't know why we moved again, but we did. We moved into a cabin with one bedroom and a coal heater in the kitchen. The stove couldn't heat the bedroom; it was so cold that when I went to check on Chuck, he was blue. I started screaming and woke Clarence up. We put Chuck in between us, and got him warmed up. We also gave him a bottle of warm milk to help warm him up inside. I was so afraid we would go to sleep and roll over on him, I never did go back to sleep that night. The next day we purchased a bassinet for him to sleep in.

Chapter Twenty-Two
The Trip Home

It wasn't long before the servicemen got recalled back to active duty. Clarence hitchhiked to Salt Lake City, Utah and was reassigned to a military base in Georgia. I didn't have any money to go home on, so I had to write home for some.

After the money came, I packed up my clothes and the baby's things, made about six bottles of milk, (he was a Carnation Evaporated Milk baby, which meant that the evaporated milk mixed with water), took some extra cans of milk for the trip, put the baby in the bassinet, and went down to the bus station for the long trip home to Kentucky. In about two hours we were back in Missoula, Montana.

The cab driver, which took us from the bus station to the train station, started to put the bassinet in the trunk with our other belongings. Another girl was in the cab, too.

She told him, "You idiot! There is a baby in there."

Once we were on the train, Chuck slept most of the way. There were servicemen on the train, also. They all wanted to take turns holding him, it was the innocence of a child, I believe. One said he wanted to hold the "big baby," and everyone laughed. A sense of great pride rode with me that day, to bring joy to the men going back off to fight in the war.

One of the civilians on the train stopped and looked at Chuck and then told me that even though the baby looked at me, he couldn't actually see me. It made me mad. I would talk to Chuck and he would smile at me.

I told the man, "Look, he does see me."

Another young man that was with the man said, "Don't pay him any mind."

I asked him how come he wasn't in the service. He told me they were actors and were entertaining the servicemen.

When we got to Chicago it was dark, and I had to wait for the next train to Cincinnati. They had beds in a nursery for women who were traveling with babies.

One of the women in there told me, "You should put your baby in one of the beds."

I don't know why, but I remember thinking she was crazy if she thought I was putting my baby in one of those beds.

I kept him in the bassinet and went back into the station where there were long benches. I put the bassinet down and lay down in front of him. I didn't mean to, but I finally went to sleep. Sometime later, a woman woke me up and told me my baby was crying. Naturally, I was startled, but I did manage to thank her and took care of his needs.

Finally we got on the train heading for Cincinnati. When I went to give Chuck a bottle, I found that the milk had soured. Checking the other bottles, I found they were all sour. The train conductor told me I could go use the kitchen and fix him some more formula, and that he would watch the baby while I was gone.

I went to the kitchen, washed and scalded all the bottles, and made new formula. Most of the men who worked in the kitchen were black. They had big smiles on their faces and were very friendly.

Once we arrived in Cincinnati, I knew we were on the last leg of the trip. Back on the coal-burning, cinder-spitting, black-smoking and loud open-windowed train, heading for the Appalachian Mountains, the place I called home, and that I always came back to. It was all I could do to keep my baby clean.

The wet diapers I would rinse out, and the messy ones I just tossed down the toilet onto the railroad tracks. There were not train stations.

If you wanted on or off the train, you just stopped it. I had run out of evaporated milk by now. At the next stop I went to a store to buy more milk. I also got some oranges to make orange juice for him to drink. The owner wouldn't take my money, but he did take some of my ration stamps. He explained that he couldn't buy any more milk without them.

Back then, news traveled faster than the trains did. Somehow my mother knew that I was coming home and would be on the next train. There was talk in town that a woman on the train was traveling with a baby, and about what good care she gave him. They talked about how she had even made the baby some orange juice to drink along the way. My mother said she knew it was me they were talking about, even before I got there.

Geraldine – 1944
21 Years Old

Chapter Twenty-Three
Back Home with Chuck

Life in the old house never did change, and our father remained the same. Every weekend he would go out and get drunk. Sometimes he would come home and just go to bed. Sometimes he would make us get up and fix him something to eat. This was not an easy thing to do; there wasn't fast food back in those days.

We would have to get up, build a fire in the coal stove, peel potatoes and fry them. If we had meat, we had to cook it, too, and maybe put some eggs alongside. Sometimes he would eat it and sometimes he would just fall face-first into it.

One night he came home with a gun. We were all afraid to even come down the stairs. We crawled out onto the rooftop, over on the other side where the hill was, and jumped down. We went next door and stayed with the neighbors. I wouldn't go into the house. I just sat in their yard on the swing, holding my baby in my arms, thinking about how much I hated my father.

When daylight came, my sister, Magdalene, crawled on her hands and knees into the house and got the gun away from him, he didn't even miss it. The things he did to us were endlessly just plain wrong.

One day we missed the baby. My little sister, Cat, who was baby-sitting, took him over to Barn Hill. She was about ten years old. When she didn't come back right away, we went looking for her. We met her coming back with the baby. It was all she could do to hold onto him.

She said, "I just took him to see Aunt Pearl."

Well, Aunt Pearl lived at least a mile from our house. I didn't say anything to her at that time, because the baby was all right.

My mother told her that she should never have done that, and asked her, "What if you would have dropped him?"

Cat cried and said, "All I wanted was for Aunt Pearl to see him."

I remembered that when she was a baby I used to carry her into the hills. I had probably been only about twelve years old at the time, and she was just a baby. So I couldn't get too terribly mad at her for taking Chuck to see Aunt Pearl.

Then there was the time I laid Chuck on the bed next to my mother, and he started to kick. He kicked her arm, and she said, "Geraldine you are going to have to move him before he kills me." She had crippling arthritis and always remained in pain, I felt bad, as she just kept rubbing her arm.

After that, whenever I put him on her bed I made sure he couldn't kick her. My mother had always said she didn't think she would ever live to see her grandchildren. She did live to see one of them, Chuck. (She has many others, now.)

She died not long after that. My sister, Magdalene, had gotten married and left. Brother, Jim, also left and went into the service. And as soon as I had a chance to get out of there, I did too.

James R. Oxford, Jr. (Jim)

Ruby, a friend from long ago, came home to Dunham for the funeral of her little brother. After the funeral she extended the invitation to go home with her to Florida. She had three little girls at the time and it didn't take much to convince me. I took Chuck and went.

Florida was great after living winters in Kentucky. We would take the kids and go: to the beach, to the zoo, the monkey jungle and the park. Sometimes her husband, Harvey, would watch the kids and we would go downtown to a place called Flagler Gardens and dance with the servicemen.

Chapter Twenty-Four
After the War

In 1945 I was still in Florida when WWII ended. Chuck was one and a-half years old, I packed us up and we went home.

Clarence would not stay up at Dunham with us, so we went to Jenkins to live with his parents. In about three months I was pregnant again. Clarence had started treating me with indifference, and I didn't know what the matter was.

When I would try to talk to him he would say, "Nothing's the matter. It's just you."

I packed my suitcase and put it under the bed. I had made up my mind to leave him.

His mother, Dora, came upstairs and talked to me.

She said, "Geraldine, honey, don't you go. You might be pregnant."

Of course I was – with my second son; John Russell Morefield was born in the hospital in Jenkins, Kentucky. She spoke with Clarence and told him that I was leaving. He came up and pulled the suitcase out from under the bed and confronted me, wanting to know why? He had all kinds of excuses for his bad behavior, and I believed every last one of them.

The Coal Company had given him a job in the mines. When he would get his paycheck he would give his mother money and thought she was saving it for us. He was a selfish man with his money. When I needed something he would not let me have any extra, only just as much as I absolutely had to have.

In the meantime, I was getting as big as a cow and needed maternity clothes. He did let me have enough money to buy material for two dresses, and his mother made them for me. Only thing was she put buttons up and down the front, and after a few months I was gaping up and down the front of my dresses.

I had not been to the doctor yet. I could not because I didn't have anything to wear. Pregnant women always want to clean up before they go the to doctor's office.

Again, his mother talked to him. He went to Neon, KY and bought me a dress. It looked like a big, checkered tent. It was wine-colored and he thought it was pretty; I was ashamed of it, but I wore it anyway and went to the doctor. Thank God I was healthy! That was the only time I saw Dr. Perry.

John Russell Morefield
Born August 26, 1946 in Jenkins, Kentucky

I had Johnny at the Jenkins Hospital where the doctors and nurses could take care of us. When I left the hospital, my father-in-law, Mr. Morefield, came and got Johnny and me. He carried his grandson all the way home; with the biggest smile and sense of pride I had ever seen. While Johnny was in the nursery, people would come to see me and tell what a beautiful baby he was. My sister-in-law, Lucille Cantrell, came to see us.

She said, "Geraldine, you have the prettiest baby in that entire nursery."

There were about seven babies in there. I got out of bed to go and see for myself. I held onto the walls going there, but it was worth the trip. He WAS a beautiful baby, and by the time he was 9 months old, he could walk.

It was crowded with all of us living in that house. There were seven of us and sometimes as many as ten. We all worked hard keeping it clean and we got along just fine. When we were done with our work at the end of the day, we would sit on the back steps and talk. That is, everyone except Clarence. He would be at the pool hall or playing cards somewhere else.

They started the lay-offs in the coalmines. Some of the men left and went to West Virginia. Clarence didn't wait for them to lay him off; he went to Logan and got a job in one of the mines there. On weekends he would come home with his dirty clothes in his suitcase and a couple of bottles of beer for me. I washed his clothes while he went and played cards or pool. Then he would leave on Sunday evening, going back to Logan.

When he'd leave, his mother would ask, "Geraldine, honey, did Bud give you any money?"

I would have to tell her, "No," and ask her, "Why?"

She would tell me that she had seen his script card, and that he was drawing all his money out to go gambling.

This went on for two years, between 1948 and 1950. By then, Chuck and Johnny were two and three years old. Clarence stopped coming home every weekend, and then he just stopped coming home all together. I went next door and asked Tinnier Daniels if I could clean her house, do her washing and ironing, so that I could make enough money to buy bus tickets to go to West Virginia with my children. I don't know what I thought I was going to do when I got there, but I was determined to go.

I made enough money to order Chuck and Johnny clothes from a mail-order company. I bought material for a gray suit for myself, and a woman who still lives in Jenkins to this day, Delores Farley, made the suit for me, as well as a pretty silk blouse from material she had, and gave to me.

I am always thankful to people who have showed me kindness, especially my mother-in-law, Dora. She was always good to me and treated us like her own. Both she and Jess tried to get Clarence to do right by his family.

The day I left to go to West Virginia, Dora told me, "Geraldine, when you get up there, you tell Bud I said for him to make a home for you and these children." She had a sweet soft voice that was never raised in tone or harshness.

On the trip, Chuck got carsick and threw-up on the man sitting next to me. Both of my boys were on my lap because they would not sit on the seat by themselves. When we got there, Clarence met us at the bus stop. He had on a new red and white-checkered sweater. We went to a cheap hotel to spend the night. It was so bad that the bed sagged in the middle without anyone even on it.

I asked him, "Why are we staying here

He said, "It's all I can afford."

He claimed we couldn't go where he was staying because the lady he was renting from wouldn't let us stay there because we had children. He thought I had gone to all this trouble just to come for the weekend.

When he mentioned my going back to Jenkins, I told him, "Clarence, your mother said for you to make a home for our children and me."

He turned pale. He couldn't believe his mother had said that.

He asked me, "Did she really say that?"

He told me he couldn't find a place right then, and so he took us to where he was staying to see if the landlady would let us stay the night.

It was a big, old, white house. He explained to the landlady what had happened, and asked if we could stay until he found another place. She knew about a basement apartment that was vacant and told him about it. And, she did let us spend the night in the room he was renting.

During the night I had to get up to go to the bathroom. It was out on the porch, and in order to get there I had to go through the kitchen. When I turned the kitchen light on, I was shocked. There were rats as big as cats on the table, eating food. When I turned the light on, they ran in every direction.

The next morning, she fixed breakfast for us on that same table. I was half-afraid to eat. I asked her if she knew about the rats, and she said, "Yes," like it was nothing.

Clarence rented the basement apartment, and put us back on the bus to Kentucky to get the rest of our personal things. While I was there, Dora told me that Clarence had not helped with anything. We had all been living off what little his father, Jess Morefield, got from Social Security and what his sister, Betty, had given her mother to help out.

I told her that Clarence had told me that he was keeping the whole family, and that was why he didn't have any money for us. She said, "Geraldine, honey, he lied. He has gambled all his money away." Still, I took the boys and went back to West Virginia. Had I known what was in store for us, I would never have left Mrs. Morefield's house.

Chapter Twenty-Five
The First Years in West Virginia

The basement apartment had one bedroom with a bed and a dresser. The kitchen had a table, stove and one single cabinet. The bathroom was in the hall outside, which we shared with another couple. Living in the basement was hard on us. It made me hurt between my shoulders all the time, from the dampness and cold. We moved in there in the fall of the year.

The only time we got out was when I would take Chuck and Johnny and go for a walk on a road that went around the side of the hill. Clarence would do the grocery shopping, and he would have me make a list of what I needed. Then he would walk over into town, do the shopping, and take a cab back.

That Christmas, we didn't have a tree or anything else that resembled a celebration of the season for the children. There was a woman in the next apartment that had cut the top of her tree off. She put it outside of her apartment in the hall. I picked it up and took it inside.

I filled an empty Maxwell House coffee can with dirt and gravel to hold the tree top up so we could have a Christmas tree for the boys. I put paper around the can and made decorations out of tin foil.

(In 1997, there were three Christmas trees in my house. That was the first time I really thought about that Christmas in the basement. I don't look back too much because you can't do anything about the past. But if you do, remember the bad times and then be thankful for the good times. I truly did appreciate my house and my Christmas trees later on in life.)

One night, while we were living there, I felt something on my head while sleeping, and it woke me up. As I put my hand up to feel what it was, I could feel it was a rat that was digging in my hair. I jumped out of bed, screaming, and turned the light on. After that, I slept with all of the lights on in the apartment. We had learned that the rats wouldn't come out while the lights were on.

Clarence worked the afternoon shifts in the coalmines, so they didn't bother him. As soon as he would get up, he ate and left to go to work. That gave him plenty of time to gamble with the men before his shift started.

In early spring, it started the rainy season, and Logan began flooding. The water would come down from the mountainsides, and would form rivers in the hollers between them, and most of the basements were always going to flood. The people who owned the house put everything up on the porches, and so did we. We knew we had to get out of the way of the water and out of that house. Clarence said we were going to Eddie's house for a while.

Eddie, his wife, and child lived in a very nice apartment. From their window you could see people going over to Logan down the railroad tracks, to find an alternative place to stay. I asked Eddie's wife how they got over there. She explained it to me. I asked Clarence if we could go over to town and find a place. He said we didn't have any money. When it came time to go to bed, Eddie's wife put Chuck and Johnny on the couch. Then she and Eddie went to bed, leaving Clarence and I sitting at the kitchen table. Sometime during the night, I couldn't sit at the table any longer. I lay down on the floor to sleep and Clarence lay down with me.

The next morning she fixed breakfast for us. Eddie and Clarence left to see if the floodwaters had gone down any, his wife and I, sat and talked awhile.

All she could talk about was how I let Clarence run my life, and how her husband talked about how Clarence lost all his money, gambling. Clarence and Eddie finally came back. They had on rubber boots, and Clarence had brought a pair for me. He told me the people we were renting the basement from said we could have the two room house that was behind that house.

Clarence carried Chuck, and I carried Johnny. We waded in mud almost to out knees to get to the house. When we got in, mud was all over the floor. We had to shovel and sweep, and throw water on the floors to get all the mud out. Meanwhile, Chuck and Johnny sat on the table.

It was so cold you could see their breath.

The gas was turned off because of the flooding, so we had no heat. We plugged in a toaster to warm our hands and crawled into bed with our coats on. We put Chuck and Johnny in bed with their snowsuits on and covered up with all the blankets we had.

Finally, we went to sleep; praying the gas would be turned on the next day.

The house had better furniture than the basement apartment. After I got it cleaned up, it wasn't so bad. At least there were windows with pretty yellow curtains in the kitchen. The bathroom was on the porch; we still bathed in a galvanized washtub, and washed clothes on a washboard.

After we moved out of the basement apartment, a middle-aged couple moved in. The woman looked like she could have been a guard in a prison. Her husband reminded me of my father. Sometime later, the landlord and his wife moved away, and the "odd couple" moved upstairs and started collecting the rent.

Chuck had a friend, a little boy who was about the same age as he was, five, and they played together. The "matron" would come around and tell me that I had to keep them boys in the back of the house, or we would have to move. She looked and acted like a crazy woman, and I had no idea what was the matter with her.

I talked to the mother of Chuck's friend, and she told me the "matron" was jealous of me because I laughed and talked to her husband. She said, "She had an empty apartment, nicer than where we were, and that we could have it." So, we moved again. This one had a washing machine.

We didn't stay there too long. Clarence went to Omar and got a job. The holler where the coalmine, houses, and school were located was called Pine Creek. The houses down in the bottom were nice and new. The house that Clarence got for us was on the side of the hill. It must have been built at the beginning of time. The walls inside were made of thin pieces of wood, called slabs. I tried papering them. It looked okay for a while, and then the wood under it would swell and split the paper.

If you've ever been in the Appalachia Mountains, there are a few of these houses still standing today. You can see some of them in "Coal Miner's Daughter." They are long, three rooms in a straight row, and each room has a door to it from the porch, as well as a back door.

This one sat on the side of the mountain, on top of stilts. They were 5-6 feet tall. When the wind blew real hard, I waited for the house to blow over. But common sense told me if it hadn't blown over by now, it probably wasn't going to just because I was in it.

It was a weathered-black color, and had two fireplaces, back-to-back. There wasn't anything to stop the wind from blowing down the chimney. We would get a down draft and pretty soon soot would blow out into the house all over everything. It would take me hours to get it cleaned up.

I had a can of white paint leftover from painting the woodwork inside. One afternoon, after Clarence left for work, I painted the front porch walls, as high as I could reach, until I ran out of paint.

The girl that lived next door told me the neighbors were betting that I was going to paint the whole house. I told her I would have if I'd had enough paint and could reach it all.

Dora and his sister Aileen and her husband Gene came to see us. They couldn't stay all night because we only had one bedroom. Johnny had asthma.

There was a big tree growing in front of the house. Dora said the tree was a cedar tree, and it was the cause of Johnny's asthma.

She said, "I couldn't believe he (Clarence) has you living like this."

I was just glad she hadn't seen the basement apartment. The reason Clarence got this house was that the rent was only $7.00 a month. That left more money for him to gamble with.

Carl, a young man who lived in the house just below us, had running water in his house and I wanted water in our house. Carl told Clarence that the Mining Company would give him the pipe, and we could connect onto his pipe. I told Clarence that I would help dig the ditch for the pipe, so I dug and dug, and Clarence shoveled.

The women in the neighborhood thought I was crazy for digging that ditch. What they didn't know was that I was tired of carrying water into the house during all kinds of weather. I even had to sit up at night and keep a fire going in order to have hot water for Clarence to bathe in after he got home from work.

After we got everything ready, and Clarence had put all the pipes together, he realized he didn't have a pipe cutter. We ended up with the pipe sticking up in the air, about six feet, in the kitchen. I just set a table under it with a water bucket on top to catch the water.

When he went to Carl's house to connect our pipe to Carl's water pipe, I told him, "Clarence you cannot connect the pipes without turning the water off." Mr. Coleman, a man in the holler, knew where to turn the main line off, and I told Clarence to get him to do it. Instead, he got down in the ditch and disconnected the water pipe. Water was going everywhere. The ditch filled up with yellow mud. It overflowed and was up to his waist. The boys were watching and laughing – and so was Clarence.

The water was running down the side of the hill into the road below. By then, everyone who lived there knew what he had done. You could see, down in the bottom of the holler where everyone lived, they were standing outside watching and laughing. Mr. Coleman was running to turn off the main water line. I didn't care; I had running water.

Chapter Twenty-Six
The Boys

Clarence bought new furniture for the living room, kitchen and bedroom, a rollaway bed for Chuck and Johnny, and even a washing machine for me. I had a garden, and had made flowerpots, crocheted, and did everything I knew how to do to make it feel homey. I cooked all the things Clarence liked, and every morning made biscuits, pork chops and gravy for him. The boys and I were happy.

Chuck was old enough to go to school, and Johnny had the whole mountainside to play on. They would nail pieces of wood together to look like airplanes, and put an eyebolt on top of them so they could slide them down a string. Then they would put one end of the string high up on a tree with the other end down below, and turn it loose, running down the hill after it, laughing and screaming.

Chuck had a hatchet and would chop wood to sell to the neighbors. When I wanted to buy some, he wasn't too happy about the idea of selling it to me, because he could get more money from the neighbors. I'd have to beg him to sell it me.

I had to carry coal and chop wood for my own fires. Once I was chopping wood under the house, and apiece flew up and hit me on the forehead. It started bleeding, and I couldn't get it to stop. I didn't have any way to get to the doctor's. Then I remembered being told that if you broke an egg open, took the white membrane out and put it on the cut, the membrane would harden, seal up the cut and stop the bleeding. And, it did!

Johnny got a hold of some cigarettes that his father had while we were living there. He took them into the outhouse to smoke. Chuck came into the house and told on him.

I said, "It's all right. Let him smoke."

We stood at the kitchen window and watched the smoke bellowing out the cracks of the outhouse. It looked like it was on fire! After a few minutes, the door burst open and Johnny fell out, coughing and gagging. He was really sick, and I felt bad for him, but, thinking back on it, it was hilarious to watch.

One summer's day the boys had been a hand full. Even though there were snakes everywhere, black snakes, copperheads, and rattlesnakes, I thought they would be safe playing out behind the house where it was cool. I told the boys to stay out of the tall grass, and sent them outside to play.

They were playing with their hammer, nails and wood. I went inside and sat down to take a break. They both came in; screaming that there was a snake out there and it had crawled out from under the house. I never will forget how big their eyes were.

One of the young men, who lived around the corner, came over with a gun. As it turned out there was not one, but three copperheads. He shot them all, right there and then!

One other time Chuck saw a rattlesnake on the coal pile. He had heard the men talking about getting rattlers off snakes, and he came in yelling and screaming about there being a rattlesnake out there and that he was going to get the rattler.

I had to do some fast explaining to him, that he was not going to do any such thing. We ended up getting the same young man to come over and shoot this snake, too. Then we allowed him to take the rattlers off the snake.

Carl was good with the boys. Once he was chopping wood, and all the kids were hanging around, laughing and talking with him. They kept throwing rocks over into the tall grass at something that was moving. They thought it was a rat. Carl took his long-handled, double-bladed ax over to look.

He started chopping, cursing, and yelling for the kids to get away. The kids were screaming and laughing, we all thought Carl was playing with them until he held up the snake. It was six feet long, and where he held it by the neck, his hand could barely reach around it, and it was a black king snake.

Then there was that day that Johnny went missing. I took off, down the hill, into the bottoms, looking for him. There was a train there, called a dinky (like a big train, only smaller). It was used to carry coal slate up the mountain for dumping. The engineer was sitting in the cab.

I asked him if he had seen a little boy, and he said, "Yes."

He said the boy was going to school. I went to the schoolhouse, and there he was, playing in the schoolyard. I picked him up and took him home. I told him, "Next year you can go to school."

Then there was the day he threatened to run away from home. It was raining. I put his little yellow raincoat on him and put him out on the front porch. He kept standing right where I put him, not moving to go at all, he was mad that I had called his bluff.

I pecked on the window and told him to "go on."

He started crying and that broke my heart.

So I went out on the porch and made him promise he wouldn't run away. He never mentioned it again.

One beautiful morning I went out on the front porch. There was Johnny, with a towel tied around his neck, standing up on top of the banister. In a real calm manner I asked him what he was doing, and he said, "Playing Superman."

Well, Superman's mother gave him a spanking when she finally got him to come down, because he was at least nine to ten feet off the ground, and if he had slipped and fallen, it surely would have killed him or at least broken his legs.

We still used an outhouse for our toilet. I wouldn't keep what was called a "slop jar" or "chamber pot" in the house. My mother told me they were "nasty." I would make sure the boys would go before they went to bed. I'd tell Chuck and John to go out on the porch and urinate through the banisters.

I would hear them laughing out there. So, one night I looked out the window to see what they were laughing at.

Instead of urinating through the banisters, they were standing out at the end of the porch, where the steps were, trying to see how high they could make it go. Sure enough, "Boys will be boys."

While we lived there, Chuck was sick a lot with his tonsils, and had to have them removed. I wanted to go to the hospital when he had his surgery.

Clarence took up playing the proud father and told me, "There is no need for you to go."

When I wouldn't shut up about wanting to go, he told me the reason he didn't want me to go was because of the men who were in the ward, and them exposing themselves. I kept it up until he gave in, and took me to see Chuck. When he saw me, he started to cry. He told me how much his throat hurt. Clarence said,

"See what you have done by coming here? You have made him cry. Come on, I am taking you home right now."

I was so embarrassed. The men in the ward were all looking at us and I just cried.

Clarence still gambled and his treatment of me was still the same. It was so bad at times; I'd kneel down by the boys' bed and pray to God to help me stay with him, for their sakes.

I knew any kind of home with him was better than what would happen if I took the boys and left. I never even thought about going back to Dora, even though I know she would have taken us in and been good to us because she loved Chuck and John, and me.

Chapter Twenty-Seven
On the Move, Again

I never understood him; I just lived with him. I would get so lonesome; because he worked afternoons and on the weekends we would leave to go play pool or cards. He didn't come home until real late at night. One weekend I asked him to stay home. He just laughed. Then I got this idea to hide his dress pants so he couldn't go anywhere. When he couldn't find them, he said, "Get my pants for me before I hurt you."

In 1952 we saved some money and bought a car, a little black 1941 Ford. Clarence had a friend named Cupid who taught him to drive. Clarence was thirty-four years old when he learned to drive. Later, he went and traded the Ford for a Chevy. It was blue and had a small seat in the back for the boys. I can remember going for a few Sunday rides in it, but mostly Clarence used it to go out on Saturday nights to watch wrestling.

The next year, in 1953, he came home from work one day and said he had quit his job and was going to Detroit, Michigan. The papers from there had ads in them wanting help in the factories to build automobiles. If you have ever seen the movie, "The Doll Maker," this was exactly what it was like for us.

He sold our furniture. Everything in the house was gone, even the car. All we had was our clothing. He paid a young couple to drive us to Jenkins.

Instead of him sitting in the back seat with us, he sat up front and kept patting my knee from the front seat, telling me, "Everything is going to be all right."

He left us, again, with his mother, Dora. Only this time, he left some money with me. It was for us to use to get to Michigan. This time I gave Dora some money to help feed us. It wasn't so bad being there, I would visit with my sisters, and Cat was living with Bootsy.

Magdalene had moved to Ecorse, Michigan, and Elmer had been there awhile. Clarence went to her house. Elmer had become a foreman at Chrysler and got Clarence a job there. I was happy to have enough money for train fare. Cat came with me, and I was happy to have her along, and she loved my boys.

It was springtime in Kentucky. The flowers were all blooming, and Mr. Morefield had his garden in. We'd already had a mess of wild greens. I left our winter coats to be mailed later. I wore a suit; the boys had new blue coat-sweaters. Cat had on a jacket.

On the train, people were carrying winter coats, and some even had them on. At the time I couldn't understand why. When the train pulled into Detroit, I found out why.

It was very cold outside and snowing.

One of the first things we did was to buy jackets and caps for Chuck and John. I wrote Dora right away to send our things.

Finding a place to live was hard, so Clarence went to a real estate office. They had this big, old house they had turned into apartments. The said we could rent the downstairs apartment if we would take care of the upstairs apartments. That included cleaning them when they were empty, as well as collecting the rent. The house was on Military off of Fort Street in the downtown area.

It had been a nice house, at one time. It was sparsely furnished. In the living room there was an iron bed. The library had built-in bookcases, a fireplace, and was used for the living room. The dining room had a bed in it. The kitchen had a table, homemade cabinets on the wall, and a gas stove from the stone ages that you had to light with matches, and it scared you every time.

Fort Street was the main street with four lanes of traffic ending up in the heart of the city. We had to cross it to get to the school Chuck and John attended. Thank God I had been out of the mountains before, or it would have been a disaster. The boys and my sister Cat, had never been anywhere but Jenkins and West Virginia. Being in downtown Detroit was quite a shock! The traffic scared the boys. If someone blew their horn, they would try to go back to the sidewalk. People stared at us. Cat and I would take them to school and go pick them up, daily.

After Cat got used to the streets, she'd say to me, "You stay home. I'll go get them." We went job hunting in our little, old, thin clothes. The wind would blow so hard we could feel it clear through our clothes. I would say to her, "Maybe when we get around on the other side of the building, it won't be so cold." But, it was. I had never been so cold in my life.

I got an interview for a job and when I went for a physical, the nurse realized I had a hearing loss. She called the doctor in the room and told him. He told me I couldn't work there because I might get hurt. We needed me to work, and I really wanted that job, cause it paid good money, so I just went home and cried.

At that time Cat was married to a young man named Tommy Sanders. At this time, he was in the Army. But, when he returned home to Kentucky, Cat went back there to join him.

Chapter Twenty-Eight
The Early Years in Detroit

By now I had made friends with the woman who lived across the street. Her name was Betty Little. Her husband's name was Buzz. They had two children; a boy named Joey, about Chuck and John's age, and a little girl.

Betty asked me, "Why don't you go to work? I told her about my hearing problem, how I had a hard time hearing some people's tone of voice. She said, "I will take you to Wyandotte, where they sell hearing aides, and we'll see how much they cost."

We went, but they were more than I could afford. When I got back, Clarence was home. He claimed that he was standing on the street corner, and we passed him right by. He said we looked right at him and laughed.

I really didn't see him, but by then I had had enough! We were eating dinner and I don't know what possessed me, but I picked up my plate of spaghetti and threw it. It hit the top of the arch over the kitchen door and I started crying. He had been laying down in the living room, mouthing off at me.

He jumped up and ran into the kitchen.

All he said was "Look at what a mess you've made." I didn't care. Betty came over the next day. Her husband had accused her of causing us to fight. He told her we were happy before she stuck her nose in our business. I told her the truth about how it really was to live with Clarence.

She said, "If you want to work, I'll take you downtown on the bus to J. L. Hudson's, and they will give you a job." I can still remember how nice Mr. Lee was. He was the man who interviewed me.

When Bootsy and Herbert came to Detroit, I took her to see Mr. Lee, and he gave her a job, too. My being hard of hearing didn't bother the girls I worked with, but some of the buyers got irritated at having to speak up. When I finally got my hearing aide, I was happy to tell them.

They got big smiles on their faces. They were happy for me, too. I sure enjoyed working there. I think I was there about seven years.

The kids on the street where we lived were tough. They would roller skate across the grass, jump up onto the porch and skate across it, ruining the grass and the porch. We were responsible for the property. There were about six boys that did this. I would ask them not to, and they would just laugh at me.

One day, Chuck and John were playing in the basement with Joey Little and a couple of other boys. I had told them not to let anyone else in the basement. Well, after awhile Chuck came out of the basement. He had been beaten up.

I asked him, "What happened?" He said, "You told us not to let anyone else inside and that boy, Frank, came to the cellar door. I told him he couldn't come in. So, he beat me up."

I went down to Frank's house to tell his mother what he had done. He stood there and told his mother that he had never seen me before. His mother was sitting on the steps, smoking a cigarette. She said, "Well, you heard what he said, didn't you?"

I couldn't believe my ears. When I was a child, if you did something you weren't supposed to and a neighbor came and told your parents, you got punished.

Well, I went back home, but the next time they started on my boys, I just picked up the telephone and called the police. The police went down to talk to their mothers. Their mothers told the police that if I had just come down and talked to them, they would have made the boys stop.

Clarence was hiding in the house saying, "You're going to get us in trouble."

I did, but not the kind he was talking about. The two policemen would drive by to check out those boys, making sure they weren't causing any more trouble. I would be out front, with the water hose, cleaning off the porch and the walkway. They would even stop to talk with me, asking about Chuck and John.

Once, one of them asked me to go out with him. I didn't know what to think. I just stood and looked at him, turned around, and went straight into the house. They never did stop again, but they would wave when they went by. I grew up thinking policemen were "White Knights in Shining Armor," and I still like to think of them that way.

I started a savings account at the bank, on the corner across from Hudson's. Almost every week I made a deposit of $30. Hudson's paid us in cash. I got $32. I used the two-dollar bill for my $1.75 bus tickets. I carried my lunch most every day.

Clarence had told me if I would save the down payment, he would buy me a house in Lincoln Park. Of course I found out, years later, that we didn't need a down payment, we could have used his VA benefits.

Chuck and John

Chapter Twenty-Nine
Hillbillies and City Slickers

I bought the boys roller skates, running along beside them until they learned to skate. When Christmas came, I got them ice-skates, and ran around the outside of the ice rink in Clark Park until they learned to skate on them.

At Christmas time I would take them downtown to Hudson's. They had "Toy Land" on the 13th floor. There were animated toys for the children to see. It was a "first" for us, and we were amazed. I would also take them up to the 18th floor, where you could look out the windows and see the Detroit River, Belle Isle, and over to Windsor, Canada.

We would go out on the boat to the island, which was an amusement park, and dance on the boat. They had a band for music, and we had packed a picnic lunch. It was the first time Chuck and John had ever been to an amusement park, and they had a great time running and riding all the rides.

I had a great time just watching them enjoy the day and be children.

We also went to the theater on Fort Street. It was one of those big, old theaters they used to have. It was truly beautiful to look at. We always thought Clarence was at the pool hall, but sometimes we would run into him at the theater.

The first time that happened, I was surprised and hurt, thinking he would go and not take us. After the hurt went away, I didn't care. They boys would have puzzled looks on their faces when they saw him there. I couldn't explain to them why, because I didn't know why, myself.

The people that rented the apartments, upstairs, started complaining that there were bedbugs in the beds. We told the Realtor, and he sent an exterminator to get rid of them.

The exterminator explained to me that the bedbugs were "southern" bedbugs, that the hillbillies who moved up to Detroit brought them. He said there was a difference between "southern" and "northern" bedbugs.

I just stood there and listened to him tell me this, all the while getting madder and madder.

Finally, I asked him, "Just how can you tell it's a 'southern' bedbug? Does it say, "Y'all

– Or – you'ins?"

He got red in the face and left.

Chuck and John came home from school, one day, all upset.

They asked me, "Are we *hillbillies*?"

I asked, "Why?"

"Well, the kids outside say we are," they answered.

I told them, "Yes, we are, and it's nothing to be ashamed of." Now you go right back outside and call those kids "*city slickers*."

In a few minutes I could hear them yelling, "CITY SLICKERS! CITY SLICKERS!"

It did my heart good!

On this particular day, the sewer had backed-up into the basement. I had never seen anything like it. It was all over the floor and up into the shower. When the water drained off, it left all the mess behind. I don't know how it became my job to take a push broom and push it all back into the drain, but it was, and I did. Then I washed down the basement and the shower/bath area with Lysol disinfectant.

The next day, when I got home from work, there were men from the city digging up the street.

The sewers had stopped-up all the way to the street. The woman, who lived in one of the upstairs apartments, had been throwing sanitary napkins into the toilet, plugging up the whole sewer system.

I told Clarence, "You tell the Realtor that if this happens again, we are moving."

Well, it did happen again, and I did not clean it up that time.

I told Clarence, "You push it down the drain and clean up the mess, or move."

We went down Fort Street to the Fort Clark Apartments, and asked the landlady if she had an apartment we could rent. She only had a two-room one, with a Murphy bed. She said we could have it, and when one of the three-room apartments came empty, we could move into it.

We didn't have anything to move, just the clothes we had. Clarence went to a furniture store and got a couch that made into a bed, some chairs, and a breakfast set. We moved into the apartment. The Realtor told Clarence,

"Your wife really meant what she said." What he didn't know was that Clarence wasn't about to clean that mess up, and I refused to.

The apartments on Fort Street were painted nice and had hardwood floors, incinerators in the halls, elevators, and washers and dryers in the basement. I could catch the bus on the corner, and we were only a block from the boys' new school.

Moving meant the boys had had to change schools. Now they went to a school on Clark Street, which was also where the park and the YMCA were. They didn't have to go across Fort Street anymore to go to school. We would go to the park, and I would rent bikes for them to ride.

They brought home cards from the YMCA. Every week I'd give them some money so they could join the YMCA and take swimming lessons. Every time, Clarence would be on my case that they were going to drown, and it would be my fault.

I talked to one of the women I worked with about it. She told me the YMCA was the best place they could be. She said there was a lifeguard there that would take good care of them while they were swimming.

When the boys learned to swim, they invited the parents to come and watch. I was real proud of them. The parents would throw money into the pool for the kids to dive for and retrieve. John looked like a frog in the water. He was a really good swimmer one of the best there. It was like walking or breathing to him, he was a natural.

Later, the YMCA taught them to make sailboats, and to sail in contests. In one of them, Chuck won a ribbon for sailing his from Belle Isle. His picture was in the Detroit newspaper and I kept it for years. The boat disappeared later on after he grew up and moved away. He still swears his little sister, Sharon, took it down to Swan Creek in Newport and sunk it. She denies this allegation to this very day.

Chapter Thirty
The Next Move

We hadn't been in the nice apartment too long and Clarence came home one night, ready to move again. He was now working at the Cadillac plant off of Junction. He rode the bus, and he wouldn't carry a lunch. He found an apartment on the corner of Clark Street and Toledo, alongside the storefronts there.

It had two bedrooms, and it was within walking distance to his work. Our door opened out onto the sidewalk, where there was a stop sign. The apartment needed painting, and the bathroom didn't work. The lady who owned it gave me some paint, and helped Clarence fix the bathroom.

There was a house, next door, with a walk between us. The only window we had was in our bedroom. It was on the side next to the house and walkway. People from the street would go in-between the houses. And, there were gangs, always going up and down the sidewalks. Behind the stores there was a yard where people burned their trash in big oil drums.

The man, next door, would offer to pay the boys to burn the trash, and the woman would say,

"I'll pay them more not to burn it."

The boys had to change schools again. Counting Pine Creek, this made four schools within a short period of time. It was always very hard on them, leaving their new friends behind.

I had made up my mind that I was not washing any more on a washboard. Clarence told me I could go to Gardner White Furniture Store and get a used washing machine. The salesman told me that for a few dollars more I could have a new one and a lot of free Tide detergent. I gave him what I had, and went home to tell Clarence.

Clarence became angry and told me, "I told you to buy a used one. Now go back up there and get what I told you to get."

I went back and told the salesman.

He said, "These are used washers, and they are no good. I really don't want to sell you one."

I then explained, again, that my husband told me I couldn't have a new one.

They delivered the machine that cost $42.00. After a few loads, the wringer stopped working, and I had to wring everything out by hand, anyway.

Someone gave Chuck and John a couple of white dogs that looked like little hounds. We really had no way to keep them, but the boys were happy to have them. Clarence and I would go to work, and the boys would go to school. The dogs were alone in the house and used the throw rugs for their business. It wasn't long before they had to go.

Chapter Thirty-One
The Car

By this time I had managed to save close to $3,000.00, and Clarence started talking to me about how much better off we would be if we had a car. He told me we needed a car because we couldn't even go house hunting without one.

He said, "You can always save more money for a house. And, we could go home to Kentucky for a visit, and take the boys to see their grandparents."

As usual I gave in; besides, I was really homesick it had been along time since we were with family. So we purchased a 1955 Bellaire Chevy, drove down to Kentucky, and visited with everyone, and we all had a very nice time.

Every day Clarence would wash the new car. He even found a garage for it. On the weekends I would beg him to take us to Belle Isle. Sometimes, when I absolutely insisted, we would actually take us.

He loved to swim, and he would swim around the island in the middle of the Detroit River.

I begged him to teach me, but he would just laugh and swim away. The boys knew how to swim, so they showed me what they could – dead-man's float and a few other things.

I got to where I could float on my back, and do the breaststroke. In my youth I had never been allowed to swim due to my ear problems. I enjoyed it.

Chuck had a friend, named George Evans, and he would ask his father if George could go with us because the boys would rent canoes and paddle around the island together. Most of the time Clarence would say,

"No," because he didn't want to be bothered.

I wanted to learn how to drive, so I asked Clarence to teach me. I already knew that if you let out fast on the clutch and give it the gas at the same time, it would stall. But, that is what he kept teaching me to do, so I never could learn how to drive it. It wasn't that I couldn't learn to drive; it was that I had a bad teacher.

He didn't want me to learn to drive, because that would have meant I would be free from his bondage.

If things went wrong between us, he would jump in the car and take off.

I told him, "Any time we have a problem, and all you do is jump in the car and leave."

He slapped my face as hard as I think he could, and then did exactly what I said he would do.

He jumped in the car and left.

When we first got the car, I would help him wash and clean it. After awhile, I didn't help anymore.

I thought to myself, "Why should I?"

I didn't drive it; hardly ever rode in it, except to get groceries once in a while. But I was able to ride to the hospital in it, to have my baby, and bring her home in it. That was good.

After visiting Kentucky we headed back home to Michigan. Jimmy, Clarence's brother, and his friend, Richard Litts, came back with us. They slept on the couch, and both of them got jobs, working in Wyandotte. With his new job, Richard moved out of the house. Chuck and John liked having their Uncle Jimmy and Richard stay with us.

The men would play with them. After awhile, we heard that Richard went back to Kentucky. He didn't really like Michigan.

One day, Clarence told me, "You tell Jimmy you want him to move out."

I was surprised. I thought he was happy to have his brother living with us. When I told Jimmy he would have to move, it hurt his feelings. Tears welled up in his eyes. He wanted to know what he had done.

I wasn't going to take the blame for doing this to him, so I told him the truth. Neither one of us could understand Clarence's motives or his reasons.

Mrs. Morefield wanted to know if Clarence had said anything to Richard, and if that was the reason he had come back home to Kentucky. She said, "She would be ashamed if he had, because the Litts were one of the nicest families in Jenkins."

I had a few hundred dollars left. I knew I had made a big mistake by using my savings to buy the car. So, I went to the furniture floor in Hudson's and bought a lime oak bedroom suite and a set of Club Aluminum pots and pans. After telling Clarence what I had spent the rest of the money on, he got the message.

Chapter Thirty-Two
John's Trip to Belle Isle

I came home from work one day to find John missing. Chuck told me he didn't know where John was. I went with him to all the houses of the children he played with, but no one had seen him. I called the police. They sent an officer over. He searched the house.

I asked him, "Why are you searching here?"

He said, "Sometimes kids get into and under things, and go to sleep."

I called Clarence.

When he got there, the first thing out of his mouth was "What have you done now?" The policeman just looked at him. Then he went and got in his car, driving up and down the streets looking for John.

In the meantime, the lady who lived next door came over. She told us that she owned one of the basement apartments, and the tenant's son, Dale, was missing too. It was getting dark.

After awhile, the police brought John home. He sure was a sight to see. He was sunburned, and the tongues of his shoes were hanging out from walking so much. I hugged him, and just cried with joy. The officers had seen Dale and John coming off the end of a bridge that went over to Belle Isle. They were on their way home.

The officers hugged John and talked to him. He told them that Dale and he were talking about Belle Isle, and that Dale had never been there. He decided to take him to see it.

Clarence said he would whip him.

I said, "Oh, no you won't."

And, that was the end of that discussion. I was just happy he was safe and back home. The officers told Clarence there was no need to whip the child. John had no idea that it was at least 10 miles to Belle Isle, from our house. It was an all-day-trip.

Chapter Thirty-Three
Babies

The lady we were renting the corner apartment from said her son wanted to move into our place, so we moved back to the Fort Clark Apartments. This time we had a bedroom set and a Murphy bed.

My sister, Beatrice (Bootsy), and her husband, Herbert Winchell, came up from Kentucky and got an apartment in the same building. Gloria Ann (Cat) and her son, Gregory Allen, who had been born after she went back to Kentucky, came, too.

Bootsy and I were both expecting. My sister, Magdalene, had her baby girl, Sandra Ilene, in July. (She and Elmer ended up having 12 children total). I had my baby girl, Sharon Kay, in September, and Bootsy had her baby girl, Victoria Lynn, in October. (It must have been a cold winter, that year!)

It was most enjoyable – all us sisters being pregnant at the same time. None of us got fat-fat. We just gained weight with the babies; we all had big bellies. After we had the babies, we all went back down to our normal sizes.

Chuck and Johnny were 11 and 13 when I got pregnant with Sharon. I didn't know what they would think about my having a baby around the house.

So, one day, while ironing clothes in the kitchen, I asked them, "Have you ever thought about your mother having another baby?"

They looked at each other, shrugged their shoulders and said, "Okay. Can we go down to the park and play now?"

I told them, "Yes," and then I told them there was going to be a baby.

I was still working, and Bootsy said she would watch me get on the bus to go to work, and be there to watch me get off. She was wishing she could be as healthy as I was. She had been married about twelve years – and was going to have a c-section.

She would cry and say, "I can't never do anything right."

I told her, "Bootsy, honey, just be glad you are having a baby. It's just about the best thing to ever happen to you!"

Chapter Thirty-Four
Hudson's

When I went to J. L. Hudson's to work; the first job I ever had was checking the merchandise when it came in. Keith would cut the boxes open and set them on tables. There were about six of us who would take out the coats and dresses, put them on hangars, and count them. Then they needed someone to help in the department where they made the price tags. We put them on the clothes.

Much later, my boss decided to put me in the fur department, upstairs on the first floor. For a few days, I was content there, but I started missing the girls I was used to working with. I asked if my transfer was due to my pregnancy. My boss told me that wasn't the reason.

She said she had singled me out because of my handwriting. In the fur department, all the tickets had to be hand-written, and she told me I had the best handwriting of any of the girls in my department.

I didn't believe her, so she showed me some of the other girls' handwriting. I did have the best. But, I asked if it would be all right if I went back to my old job, and they let me transfer back downstairs.

While I worked for her, she had cancer and had to go to Grace Hospital in Detroit. Only a few of the girls that were close to her went to see her. I had been wearing this perfume, named "Evening in Paris," and it was killing her.

She never did say anything to me about it, but one of the girls told me, and I changed to something else, hoping that wouldn't bother her. They never did say what type of cancer she had.

When I got on the bus in the morning, I could hardly wait for it to get downtown. It was an exciting place, to me; everyone was always in a hurry. When I first started working, I walked at my own pace – slow -.

Then I noticed everyone passing me by. They walked with purpose, running to catch the streetlight, running to catch the bus, always in a hurry. Soon, I was doing the same thing.

I really enjoyed my work. I got to listen to the buyers talk about their buying trips to New York, and all about the new styles. They would talk about where they stayed, what they did, and they would talk about their expense accounts.

I would think, "They get paid to do this?" Some of the men were good looking, and when they came to see if their orders had come in, all the girls would get excited.

The store was beautiful. A lot of dark, rich-looking mahogany wood, with huge crystal chandeliers hanging over the jewelry department counters. The elevators were very plush and had operators in nice suits, with relaxing music playing in the background.

Sometimes I would go to work early. The doorman knew me, and since I knew where the light switches were, he would let me in to turn things on and do whatever needed to be done before the store opened. Whatever the buyers needed, we would have to do.

In the winter it would get dark early. And, at five o'clock, when I would get off work, all the downtown lights would be on. Especially at Christmas time, it was a winter wonderland.

I remember this one particular evening; it had gotten very dark. All the lights were on, and it was snowing one of those soft, white, large flakes, slow snows that just float down ever so gently. It gave me such a feeling of happiness and peace. I hadn't felt like that in a very long time.

Sometimes I even took time to stop window shop. Once I saw a color of nylon hose that I thought was so pretty. It was called "Cinnamon". It would make your legs look suntanned, and I wore that color for years.

I finally realized how bad the old gray coat I had bought in back 1946 in Kentucky looked. It was so worn; it looked like it should have been thrown away. So I went down to the coat department to get me a new one.

I found this pretty blue coat that buttoned up and down the front, with no collar. There was a buyer there who knew me. I had worked for her, and she marked the coat down because she knew I wanted it.

I kept it in her office until I had the full amount of money to purchase it. I got a white scarf and a pair of white gloves to go with it. Oh yes, and a pair of red shoes. With the old gray coat gone and a new blue one to wear, my feelings about myself started to improve dramatically.

If I saw a dress I liked, I would wait until it was marked down, and buy it. If any of the buyers found out I liked something, they would mark it down ever more, just for me. This made me feel real special and well liked.

By then, I had also started buying myself shoes. When Baker's had a shoe sale, I was right there. Their prices were right, and I could afford them. I started this love affair for pretty shoes, back then, and you know – I still have it.

(So, my daughter, Sharon, and her daughter, Bobbi Jo, and her daughter Tasia Jo, they all come by their love for pretty shoes and high heels, naturally.)

The best coat that I ever had was a gray, imitation-mutton fur coat. This woman had bought it, tailored it to fit by hemming it up two inches, and then decided she didn't want it.

They marked it down for a month's end sale, and it was my size, I felt really lucky.

One summer, the girls invited me to go out to lunch with them. They were going to this Bar & Grill to have quarter-pound hamburgers. I took their advice and ordered one off the menu.

When they arrived and we started eating them, I realized the meat was almost raw. I thought they were insane to eat them. They said they were good, prepared like that, and I accused them of being cannibals.

I wasn't going to eat raw meat, so one of the girls called the waiter over and told him to "burn" mine. They tried to keep me quiet from vocalizing about cannibals eating raw meat, and accused me of ruining their lunch.

J. L. Hudson's had doctors and a visiting nurse. If you called in sick, the nurse would come to your home to see you. I didn't know about the nurse, so when I called in sick, one day, with a stiff neck from sitting under the air-conditioner, and she showed up – I sure was surprised.

We had girls from other countries working with us. They hadn't been introduced to deodorants and personal hygiene. The bosses would send them upstairs to see the nurse about these types of problems. The girls would be embarrassed, and one of them told me no one had ever taught them about things like that.

When I thought I was pregnant, I went upstairs to see their doctor, because I didn't have one of my own. He was nice. He told me when my test came back; he would call downstairs and let me know. When he called, he told me my test came back positive.

I asked him, "Positive what?"

He laughed and said, "You are positively pregnant."

It's something to learn your way around in a big city. I knew I lived off of Fort Street. I knew Hudson's was on Woodward Avenue. I knew that my bus stop was on Fort Street, where the courthouses were.

I went places with the other girls, but I had never gone out anywhere by myself. When I did go with the girls, I would look at the buildings and try to remember the landmarks.

One day, at lunchtime, I was feeling pretty "froggy," and I decided to "leap." I wanted to go over to the next street, which was Griswald, because there were some shops over there that weren't like the ones on Woodward Avenue. When I got over there, I was startled to find out that I couldn't even see Hudson's. As big as the store was, I couldn't even see it from the next block over. The only comfort I had was that I knew it was there.

I kept getting braver, and soon I was going anywhere I wanted to go. My next trip was to the Farmer's Market, behind Hudson's. That was a treat! I had never seen anything like it.

At J. L. Hudson's I worked in the Women's Clothing department, so naturally I could find the prettiest dresses to wear while I was with child. I bought this pretty red, velvet dress with a white collar.

One of the buyers said he thought all pregnant women should have a red velvet dress. I took that as a compliment, and thanked him sincerely.

Another of the men buyers came down one day, and was talking to one of the girls that marked his clothes. After he had left, all the girls were crying. Story was that he had taken a new job at Crowley's.

They had him take a physical, and it turned out that he had tuberculosis and would have to go to Northville Hospital for treatments.

When I brought oranges for lunch, one of the prettiest Italian girls would want a piece of the orange rind. I told her she could have a piece of the whole orange, but she just wanted a little piece of rind. She told me that during the war, she along with other children in Italy had been sent to Switzerland.

There, where she stayed, the nuns taught them to eat the whole orange. Later, her mother married a soldier and they all came to the USA. She didn't like her stepfather. I cannot remember if she had any brothers or sisters.

She was so pretty. When we would go anywhere, men couldn't keep their eyes off of her, and they would just fall all over each other. You could see them turning their heads to watch her pass by.

When I was pregnant, she would watch me pull the crust off of my sandwiches.

She would say, "Gerry, eat it. It is good for you."

And, I would tell her, "Here, you eat it," and she would laugh at me.

After my baby, Sharon, was born, she came to see me. She said all the girls wanted to know how I was and about the baby. While she was there, Clarence was laughing and talking to her. He laughingly said to her, "How about you and me going out sometime?"

I was embarrassed to death by the way he was talking to her. I jumped in and said that he was only joking.

After he left, she told me, "Gerry, he is not joking.

A lot of men from the South go out on their wives."

Of course she meant other men, not my husband.

I got a lot of kidding about being pregnant. It had been 11 years since I had John. The buyer who liked the red velvet dress told me to tell them that I was "in the dark and couldn't see what I was doing." I thought that was funny, and so did they when I told them.

The girls at work would run over to where I was working and carry things around for me. They would try to get me to say that I wanted a baby girl.

But, I would tell them, "As long as it's healthy, it doesn't matter."

They took up a collection and bought me a baby bed, high chair, and a lot of things for the baby. On the last day of work, they took me out to lunch. They were all very nice women to know and to work with.

When Sharon was three months old, I got on the bus and took her downtown for all the girls to see. They told me how pretty she was, and how happy they were that I did have a little girl.

Keith told me, "She looks like a boy. She doesn't have any hair." A year later, I made him eat his words. Sharon had a pretty head of curly, blonde hair.

Chapter Thirty-Five
Sharon Is Born

Sharon Kay Morefield
Born September 19, 1957 in Detroit, Michigan

I went early in the morning to have my baby in the hospital. I was still in labor in the afternoon. Clarence wanted to know if I was going to have the baby. If not, he was going to go on to work. I told him to go on, and that I would be just fine.

One of the women at the apartment house was watching the boys. Later, she told me they were real worried. John had gone around telling everyone that his mother was in the hospital, having a baby.

Soon after Clarence left, they took me into the delivery room. I had gained 32 pounds, and this was "hard" labor. I kept waiting for them to give me something for the pain. With both of the boys, when the pain got bad, they had given me what was called "Twilight Sleep."

You don't actually pass out, but you can stand the pain. It made it tolerable. This time, they hadn't given me anything.

After I had had enough of the pain, I yelled at the doctors, "What's the matter with y'all? Do you believe in natural childbirth or something?" Back then, natural birthing was unheard of. The nurse had the palms of her hands on my belly, pushing down real hard, helping the baby come out.

She looked at me and laughed, saying,

"You got yourself into this mess, and you are going to stay awake and help us."

Just about as she was being born, they finally gave me something. When I opened my eyes a few minutes later, the doctor was holding her up in the air. Her eyes were wide open, her fist in her mouth, already sucking on it.

The doctor laughed and said, "Look at her, she is hungry already."

That night, after Clarence got off work, he came to the hospital to see how we were doing. I can tell you I wasn't happy to see him, but I was happy with my baby. She was healthy. She weighed 10 and ¾ pounds and her color were beautiful, it was like she had a tan with a glow.

The boys were happy when we came home. They couldn't keep their hands off of her. I had bought everything she would need before I stopped working. I had done the same for the boys, everything they would need for school.

Sharon had her first Christmas in the apartment. Clarence gave the boys money to buy their Aunt Bootsy and me something. I still have the little glass dish John gave me.

Chuck gave me a cake stand. When he got married, I gave it to his wife, Loretta Lowe.

I remember that I made the cake my mother had so loved that year. The one with boiled white icing and red cinnamon drops for decoration. My mother had always made this cake at Christmas. Carrying on this tradition and remembering her in this way was easy for me.

Chapter Thirty-Six
The Old House on Campbell

Clarence found this old house on Campbell in February of 1958 that had a backyard for the children. Once again, we moved, changing schools in the middle of the year for the boys.

The house needed a lot of work. The woman who owned it had tried to make it into a two-family house. A bath had been built under the staircase, and nothing was finished upstairs, so I put clotheslines up there to hang wet clothes on.

It was so cold, the day we moved, and now we had furniture to move as well as our personal belongings. When we got to the house, there was no heat turned on. I had the baby all wrapped up, but the boys and I were frozen. The furnace was located under the house, and Clarence couldn't light it. He left us, there in the cold house, and went to get the landlady to come and light the furnace.

We were close enough to the Detroit River that Chuck and John could walk down and go fishing. They would drag the river with a four-pronged grappling hook they had found. They would toss it into the river and pull out fishing poles, lead sinkers, and anything else that other folks had lost.

One day, Chuck was running through the backyard, laughing and hollering. He was holding up the biggest fishing pole we had ever seen. He told us it was an "ocean rod and reel", and all the men down at the riverbank were trying to buy it from him. He said he was keeping it, so that he could fish with it. Chuck loved to fish, and John followed right after him.

Next door there was a young man who liked the boys. In the spring of 1958, he wanted to take them and go to Wall Lake, up in Northern Michigan. His mother told me that he would take good care of them, so I let them go. They came home with perch, smelt, and a big turtle they had caught. They were both wet and muddy, but they did have a good time.

Nine months after Sharon was born, I was trying to get my husband's attention.

He would tell me, "You just had the baby."

Then he began leaving early for work because he had to give a woman co-worker a ride.

He told me, "She won't be up and ready, so I have to go in and wake her up."

"Innocent enough," I thought. "He loves me."

But when I would try to kiss him goodbye in the mornings, he was always in a hurry.

"You're going to make me late for work," was his excuse.

Years later, while we were driving down Junction, Chuck pointed out a woman walking that worked at the plant with Clarence. He told me that she was "father's girlfriend." I thought he was joking. As if that wasn't bad enough, Clarence had found a new way of gambling. Now he played the numbers, to go along with the cards and pool.

One day I went into the bathroom, and there was this big rat in the toilet. I slammed down the lid and put the diaper pail on top of it. In the inner city this is a common event, I later found out, anyhow I was going to drown the rat. I told Clarence what had happened. In a little while, we went to see if the rat had died and it was gone. I kept the lid closed after that, not knowing anything about how it had gotten into the toilet.

I talked to the people next door. They said it had come up through the sewer, into the house. At the end of the sewer line there was supposed to be a screen over the line to keep them out. But, there wasn't one at the end of our sewer line, and it was against the law not to have one.

The unfinished bath, upstairs, had an open pipe in it. One night a rat came up through it and into the house. I don't remember who saw it first, but I grabbed Sharon up and started screaming. Clarence got a board and put it down between the kitchen and living room, telling me to stay in there with the boys and the baby.

That rat ran and jumped over the board. I think my screaming made it turn around and run the other way. It jumped back, over the board, into the kitchen, and then into the closet in the boys' room. The closet had some boxes stacked in it, and the rat stood on top of them, making a noise that sounded like a scream.

Clarence was hitting it with the broom. It ran past him, out the door onto the porch and jumped off the porch to the yard, six to eight feet down. We left all the lights on that night, and Clarence went upstairs and stuck a bunch of old rags into the open pipe. We hardly slept at all that night because there had been a story in the newspaper that same week, telling about a rat being found eating the top of a baby's head.

I insisted we were moving that very next day.

Chapter Thirty-Seven
Henley Place

The very next day we found a development called Henley Place, located at the edge of Delray, a suburb of Detroit. We still had a Detroit address, and just across the Rouge River, was a suburb named River Rouge. That was where my sister, Magdalene, lived. All our children went to Rouge School.

This place had two bedrooms, a kitchen, living room and a dining room. Our couch and chair were both worn out, so Clarence got new furniture, again.

He bought new living room furniture, and now, with a real dining room, he also bought a dining room table and hutch, which I eventually gave to John and his wife Heather. I papered and painted the entire place, and it looked really nice and clean. There was even a small, fenced backyard for Sharon to play in.

Life went on, as usual. John skipped school once, and I gave him a whipping. He fell and broke his arm. And, he had to have his tonsils out. I told him it wouldn't hurt, and his father took him to the hospital. Later, when I went to see him, he was so mad at me.

His first words to me were "You said it wouldn't hurt!"

He was real sick. We found out that he had contracted pneumonia.

Clarence's father, Jess Morefield came to see us. His brother, Jimmy, had gone to Kentucky and brought him back. After his father left, Clarence started showing me some attention. (Sharon was two years old.)

I asked him, "Why the sudden interest?"

He said his father had told him that he should be ashamed of the way he treated me. It didn't make me feel any better about it, knowing that his father had told him how he should be treating me. It really didn't change a thing between us.

There was this big, Polish lady named Nelly who lived next door to us. She must have weighed over 200 pounds. Every day she would come into our apartment. She would sit around, smoking cigarettes, and talking about everything under the sun. She always came early in the morning and it made it very difficult for me to get any of my housework done.

Some days she was still there when the boys came home for lunch. It was very uncomfortable. I'd be fixing lunch for the boys, and I felt obligated to ask her if she wanted something to eat, too. In the south you are raised to be a gracious hostess and have polished manners.

She never once offered to say, "No, thank you." She would eat with them, and then – when her son would come home and lean over the banister hollering, "Hey, Ma" She would yell back, telling him to go into the house, get him some lunch, and go back to school.

My boys started calling me; "Ma." and I put a stop to that, right quick.

I told them, "If you don't want to call me *mommy* anymore, you can call me *mother.*"

To this day, John still calls me "mother". Chuck sometimes teases me and will say, "I want my ma."

Except for the time John had his tonsils out and had pneumonia, the boys had never been real sick as babies or growing up. But Sharon was, and I didn't know how sick she really was. She was having trouble breathing, and was hot to the touch.

I had put Vick's Rub in hot water, and made a tent, so she could breathe the vapor. It didn't help at all. I rocked her, and she still fussed. She seemed to be getting hotter and hotter, and I didn't know what to do.

She would go to sleep in my arms, but the minute I laid down with her, she woke right back up and would start fussing again. I sat up all night with her. The next morning we took her to the hospital.

I told the doctors how sick she had been.

He listened carefully and began to get a needle ready to give her a shot. I started to lay her down on the examining table.

He said, "Oh, no! Don't do that! Hold her up! Hold her up! If you hadn't held her up all night, she would have died. Your baby is seriously ill, and you have to take her over to Children's Hospital right now."

We took her there, and they admitted her. Immediately, they put her in an oxygen tent. She had pneumonia. The nurse would come in with a little shot glass, with something dark in it.

I asked her what it was. She said it was brandy. They were giving it to her to cut the phlegm and congestion.

They were so good to her, and she got better. She ended up spending a week in the hospital. When I went to see her, she would empty my purse, and then put everything back inside.

The nurses would tell me she wouldn't eat.

I'd ask them, "Are you trying to feed her?"

They'd say, "Yes."

I'd tell them, "Give her the spoon and let her feed herself."

She had always been so independent. The nurses would stand around and watch. They just couldn't believe it. She loved apple butter and butter sandwiches, so I would make her one and take it to her.

When it was time for me to leave, one of the nurses would take her for a walk, and she'd wave "bye" to me.

When something bad happens to me, I always think God is trying to get my attention. I started going back to church with all three of my children. We attend Gilead Baptist Church, off Fort Street for quite some time. Both of my boys were baptized there.

I had more of my neighbor than I could stand, so after a couple of years, one of the apartments across the street became empty, and we moved over there. I used the excuse that it was downstairs and had a bigger backyard, and it did.

It even had clotheslines outside that I could hang my laundry on.

In 1962, an apartment upstairs became empty. My sister, Bootsy, and Herbert moved into it. By this time, our girls, Sharon and Vicky, were five, and Boots's baby girl, Terry, must have been around three.

While we were living there, Cat had married a wonderful man named Mack Stajda, and they had a baby girl. Her name was Mary Ann. Not long after, they had another girl, named Connie. We always thought Cat was so lucky having a good looking, nice husband like Mack.

Bootsy got tired of living upstairs, and found a house in River Rouge. The boys helped their Uncle Herbert with the move.

Genie, a woman who lived in the project, had a dog with a litter of puppies. Collies, I think. John wanted one in the worst way, and I told him that the only way he was going to get one was to promise to take care of it. Of course, he did.

While the dog was a puppy, it was fine. Then, it got to be a big dog. It used the whole backyard as a bathroom. I had to make John clean it up. When I went to hang up clothes, the yard would need cleaning.

I would tell myself to just be careful where I stepped.

Then I'd get to hanging up clothes, and forget, stepping in one or two of the messes.

A couple of other kids in the neighborhood had one of Genie's puppies, too. Most of the dogs around there ran loose, and when the mailman came, the dogs would chase him. It was awful to watch. I had to call the dog pound to come and get ours before something happened to someone.

John came home from school, and Champ was nowhere to be found. He asked me where the dog was. I told him that I had called the pound to come and get him. I didn't think that John cared a thing about the dog, but the fit that he threw was "out of this world."

He kept telling me, "You had no right to do that!"

I tried to explain that the dogs were tormenting the mailman, and might even bite him.

He didn't care.

He went to the pound to get him back.

When he got there, the dog was already gone. He cried and stayed mad at me for a very long time.

One day Sharon went missing. I couldn't find her anywhere. She was allowed to play with Genie's little girls, but she wasn't there. I was a worried sick because we lived next to the Scott Paper Company and not too far from the shipyards on the Rouge River.

I got Clarence involved in looking for her. When he leaned over the banisters and looked down, he saw her inside the next-door apartment.

The woman who lived there had gone to work and left the door open.

Clarence said, "She was just looking and walking around in there."

What made him so mad was her not answering when we called her name. He took off his belt and whipped her. I took her into the bathroom and put her into a tub of warm water.

She cried and cried.

When I saw what he had done to her, I cried, too. I called him into the bathroom and made him take a look at her.

She had big, red welts all over her little legs.

I told him, "Don't you ever whip her again. If she needs it, I'll be the one to do it."

Both of the boys were growing up. John rode a little girl around on the handlebars of his bike. Chuck was also dating.

I would take the kids and go to church while Clarence sat in the parking lot and waited for us to come out. He would tell me that half the people he saw going in were all in the Fort Street Bars the night before.

One day, John ran into the house to tell me Chuck was in a fight. I ran outside. All the kids that lived around were there, watching. Chuck had this boy down on the ground, and was beating him badly.

They were both red in the face, and had marks all over them where they had hit one another. I reached down to pull Chuck off him, and the boy drew back his fist to hit me.

Chuck told him, "You had better not hit her that's my mother."

I told them both to stop, and they agreed. Chuck got up. One of the Collins' girls told me the other boy had started the fight. He had hit Chuck with his belt.

When we got inside, my son was crying. He was so mad at me.

He told me, "Don't ever interfere again."

He told me that this was one of the kids who used to beat him when we first came to Detroit. He had just about paid them all back, one by one.

Some of the women in the project worked at J.L. Hudson's, a very prominent department store located in the heart of Detroit. One of them wanted to know if I wanted to come back to work. It was the summer of 1962. The boys were out of school and could watch Sharon Kay for me.

The Scott Paper Company needed the land back that the apartments were built on, so they purchased the complex back, and everyone was given a notice to move. Now that I was working, I convinced Clarence that we could afford to buy a house, and that I would help pay for it.

Mr. Brown, the Realtor, took me house hunting. He kept taking me to look at these little old houses with brown brick siding.

I asked him, "Why do you keep showing me these houses?"

He said, "Your husband told me he didn't want anything over $5,000.00."

I told him, "Mr. Brown, you show me something nice, and I'll take care of Clarence."

Chapter Thirty Eight
Lexington Avenue

The house was decided upon and we purchased it. It was a really nice two-story brick home on Lexington Avenue, with four bedrooms upstairs and a finished basement. It sold for $9,800.00, and at that time it was a lot of money. The living room was connected to the dining room through French doors.

Clarence even agreed it was nice. It cost us $1.00 to move in, and the mortgage payment was $82.00 a month. I paid the utilities. Chuck bought a lawn mower to cut the grass and a hedger for the bushes.

The boys waxed the basement floor all the time so they could have parties down there. Both were in high school by now. Sharon Kay was going to Kindergarten and John would walk her to school.

Eventually John began skipping school. Clarence and I asked him to either go back to school or enlist in the service. He decided to enlist in the Marines. The recruiting officer said he wouldn't be sent to Vietnam. We had to sign his enlistment papers because he wasn't 18. Another boy, named Luther, enlisted when John did, and they came home together from San Diego.

John looked good. He had put on weight and had a very dark tan. He told me he was glad I had taken him to the YMCA, because some of the fellows in boot camp had it rough if they didn't know how to swim.

Chuck finished high school, got a job, and purchased a Plymouth Sports Fury. He started drag racing at Detroit Speedway. I remember him calling me into his bedroom one afternoon and showing me these big, old tires he had hidden in the closet.

I asked him, "What are you doing with those truck tires?"

He laughed and told me, "Don't tell the old man. These are called slicks, and they are for racing."

I didn't have a clue what he was talking about at the time. But, he started bringing home trophies from the races he won. I don't know how many trophies he had. He knew Clarence wouldn't approve, so he kept them hidden.

We started worrying about Sharon going to school in the late 60's so we started thinking about moving.

Chapter Thirty Nine
Two More Moves

Once again I called our realtor Mr. Brown, and he showed us houses all over Detroit. Clarence didn't like any of them. Finally, we went downriver to Rockwood, about 30 miles south, to look at a house right on the lakefront of Lake Erie.

He liked it, so we sold our house on Lexington and made a $500.00 profit. We used that to get into this house. It needed a refrigerator, a stove, and we bought twin beds for the bedroom meant for Chuck and John. The house only had two bedrooms. John was home on leave, and he helped us move.

After we moved down there, Chuck started teaching me to drive. I think Clarence got jealous, or ashamed, and started teaching me how to drive on his car, too. While John was still home, Clarence decided to teach him to drive as well. They were at war with each other by the time they got back to the house.

When it came time to sign the final papers for the house, the deal had fallen through. Come to find out, the house was tied up in an estate will. The mother had been married before, and the children wouldn't let them sell it. So we moved, again. They did give us our $500.00 back.

Clarence found this house in Newport, 20 miles further south of Rockwood. We moved in January, in one of the biggest snow and ice storms that came that year. This time, Clarence had to hire movers to move us. The truck slid into the yard; the drivers were frozen.

I asked Chuck, "Why don't you help them?"

He said, "Mother, that's what they are paid to do." And, he left for work.

I told Clarence, "This is the last time I am moving. The payments on this house are $65.00, and I can make it on my own, now. We are not moving anymore. If you want to leave, you can. The children and I are staying here."

I have nothing nice to say about that house. It had two bedrooms, a living room, kitchen, one bathroom, and an enclosed back porch. The house was covered in green tarpaper shingles. The kitchen had metal cabinets, and the well water smelled of rotten eggs.

We had to portage water in new 5 gallon galvanized gas cans for drinking. We found a Laundromat in Monroe, a town 20 miles further south, where we could get good drinking water from. The lot was huge, and we had no neighbors to speak of when we moved in.

I had to go to the doctors' office for some reason, and while I was there the nurse told me they were building a new shopping center in Monroe, and maybe I could get a job there. I started working at Bargain City Department Store in September of 1964.

Chuck had bought himself a new rag top corvette, and had a new girlfriend, named Loretta Lowe. On the 13th of November, in 1965, Chuck was all dressed up in a new suit. He looked great

Clarence said, "Do you know your son is getting married today?"

Chuck wouldn't look at me. I had known he was going to get married someday, but didn't know when. He and Loretta took me to work. She almost had to sit on his lap to make room for me. They told me they were going to get a marriage license. They were laughing, so I thought it was a joke, and didn't think another thing about it.

Sometime the next week I had to go to the Post Office. The Postal Matron told me she had seen in the paper that my son had gotten his license to get married.

I said, "You did?" She said, "You mean you didn't know?" Later, I asked Loretta how come we weren't invited. She said that they didn't think we would come.

Of course, despite the recruiter's promise, John did go to Vietnam. He wrote home a lot, and I answered all his letters. He would want things, and we would buy them and mail them to him. We watched the news every night, praying that he was all right. When Bob Hope was there at Christmas, entertaining the troops, we would look into the TV, trying to see him in the crowds of faces.

I sent him a fruitcake; made divinity candy and sent it wrapped in waxed paper. I didn't know how to ship it. He said it was smashed flat by the time it got there, but they ate it off the paper anyhow.

When Chuck got married, he moved into an apartment in River Rouge. That left Sharon and I alone with Clarence. He started complaining about the long ride into Detroit, where he worked, and was on me to move back to the Fort Clark apartments.

It was over. I had meant it when I told him I wasn't moving again. I had read in the paper that the Fort Clark Hotel had bought the apartments, and were renting them out to men.

I told him, *we* couldn't go there, even if I would.

He kept telling me that he would move to the YMCA on Clark Street, if no one would accuse him of deserting Sharon and me.

One day I came home from work, packed all his clothes, and put them out on the front porch with a note telling him he could leave anytime he wanted. When he got home, he brought them back into the house, unpacked them, and said, "This is just as much my house as it is yours. I am not going anywhere." He stopped complaining about his long rides.

Chapter Forty
The End of My Life with Clarence

John Russell came home from Vietnam in 1967. Sharon and I were so happy that he was home. He went right over to Flat Rock and got his driver's license, and then the three of us took off for Kentucky to visit Grandma Morefield. We had a great time.

That same year, my sister brought her family and moved in with us. A lot of men were dying in the mines, and her husband wanted out. He went to the Cadillac plant where Clarence worked, and they offered him a job. He didn't like working there, for some reason, and he ended up going to work over at the Ford Motor plant in Monroe. They made a trip back to Kentucky to bring their beds and few other things my sister wanted to have here.

I knew a few things about Clarence, and I knew he would take this opportunity leave us. I told my sister how he had tried to move us back to Detroit, and that I wouldn't go; how he had said he would leave us if no one would accuse him of deserting us. Sure enough he soon moved out, to the YMCA.

When Clarence left, I was glad. I wanted to file for a divorce. I didn't know what grounds I had. Back then; you had to have a very good reason to get a judge to grant a divorce. I hired a lawyer and told him about my life with Clarence.

After Chuck had moved out, Clarence had started doing things that I could not understand. We slept in separate beds, at opposite ends of the house. Sharon slept in my bed, with me, and I had a poodle that slept under the bed. When Clarence would come into the bedroom, the dog would start growling at him, and he would accuse me of making the dog do it.

There were no doors on any of the bedrooms. Clarence would come to our end of the house and stand in the shadows of the night, watching us sleep for hours.

Sometimes we were aware of him, and Sharon would whisper,

"Mother, what's he doing?"

I'd whisper back, "Nothing. Go back to sleep."

She was so traumatized by this that she sucked her thumb to help her fall asleep until she was 11 years old. The night Clarence moved out, we both noticed she didn't suck her thumb anymore.

Sometimes, he would get me out of bed during the night. Once he took me to the back bedroom window and pointed to a house across the field. There were people moving around in the house. He said, "it was someone "signaling" for me, and I told him it wasn't true." He finally let me go back to bed.

Another night he made me go look outside the kitchen window. He said there was a car driving up and down the road, waiting for me to come out. I told him, "Clarence, don't you know if that was someone wanting me to come out, causing all this trouble with you, I am not about to go out with him or her?" He just stood there, looking at me, and finally went back to bed.

Then there was the night he sneaked into the bedroom and struck me in the head with the handle of a loaded revolver. It was all I could do to control myself. Sharon had fallen off the bed onto the floor, and crawled under the bed. It was all a blur. I remember arguing with him, and him turning on the light and seeing my head bleeding.

He left the room and went back through the house mumbling about something. I bandaged my head and tried to comfort Sharon. The next day she kept asking me about my head, and I kept telling her it was nothing.

One time he picked me up from work and told me he wanted to show me something. He drove into the country a long ways. I didn't even know where we were. Finally, he stopped the car.

I could see a swamp on both sides of the road, and a fence.

He started talking about some man he thought I knew. I didn't have a clue what he was talking about. While he was talking, he had a knife in his hand, beating on the back of the car seat, stabbing it, telling me he ought to kill me right there and that he had his rifle in the trunk.

I knew I couldn't run off because there was nowhere to go. I started talking about Chuck and his new family.

I told him, "You remember that they are bringing the baby, and coming to our house."

He shook his head, started up the car engine, and drove home.

That was the final straw. It made up my mind that we needed to get away from him.

He was unstable.

I took Sharon to Chuck's house in River Rouge. I told him what had happened, and that I was going to my Brother Jim's house, in Florida. I would get a job and send for Sharon as soon as I could. Everyone was crying and very upset. I told him his father would come there looking for me. Then I went to Cat's house to hide from him.

Sure enough, Clarence showed up at Chuck's house and Chuck told him I was at Cat's. He told Chuck he was sorry for what he had done. When they drove up in front of Cat's house, she called the police. She knew Clarence had a gun. The police made Clarence put his hands on the car, and searched him for it. Chuck told the police his father didn't have the gun, and begged me to go home. I got into the car and told Chuck how his father had been acting.

After he moved out of the house, he would come over at night, pull into the driveway and sound his horn for Sharon to go out to see him. He would tell her to ask me if I would talk to him.

My sister would say to me, "Don't you go out there. He has a gun and he intends to kill you."

I was afraid, and I didn't go.

She would also say, "I have a gun. I am going to sit here, with it between my legs, and if he tries to come through that door, I will shoot him."

After awhile, he stopped coming out to the house late at night.

When I told the lawyer all of this, he said Clarence was dangerous. That is how I got the divorce, on the grounds of "mental cruelty." The divorce finally brought an end to my life with Clarence King Morefield, Sr.

Chapter Forty-One
Richard Ponto Comes/Bootsy Leaves

When I got my divorce, the department manager I was working for, Richard Ponto, asked me out to dinner. No one approved, but I really didn't care, so I went. When I came home, my sister was waiting up for me. She let me know she did not approve of it either.

Richard would come to the house sometimes, and visit. After a little while, John would say, "Don't you think it's time you left?" I would grab hold of Richard to stay, and he would say, "I was just leaving, John."

And, then he'd go. I asked him later, why he would always go, and he said,

"I don't want to cause any trouble." I thought it was ironic. Here I was, in my mid-forties with grown children. Did I really need to ask permission?

When my sister was ready to move, Richard drove her around house hunting. She found a house on Woodland Beach and moved there. John got a job at the Ford plant in Monroe, and moved. Once again, it was just Sharon and I, alone in the house in Newport.

Richard was the kindest person I had known in a long time. He was good to me. He would take Sharon and I on trips to northern Michigan to see places and things we had no idea were there. One of the best was to Indian River to see an 80-foot tall cross of Jesus Christ.

We went to the sand dunes in Muskegon, a lot. He would go pick up his two children, Larry and Laura, and we would all go to the park with them. We would cook, fish, swim, and enjoy ourselves. I never laughed so much in my entire life. We went to Cedar Point, in Ohio, and over to Canada for Sunday drives.

Sometime later, Richard asked me to marry him. I didn't have the money to buy anything to get married in, so he bought me a beige knit suit and a brown suede coat. The day we got married, he gave me roses to wear. The couple that witnessed our marriage went with us to dinner.

I asked John to watch Sharon for me as we were going up north for a weekend honeymoon. It started snowing, and we only got as far as Flint.

In 1971, Richard started working at the Chrysler Engine plant, in Trenton, and I started working at a factory in Newport, called B & M Stamping. I was running a punch press. After I got married, my sisters wouldn't have anything to do with me.

That same year, about the first or second week in November, my sister called to tell me Bootsy was in the hospital. She had had surgery and they found out she had cancer. To tell the truth, it didn't bother me much. I thought, "Why is she telling me this? They haven't had anything to do with me for over two years."

The next day, her daughter Vicky called me. She said Bootsy had terminal cancer, that she was going to die, and her mother wanted me to come to the hospital. That got my attention. I went to the hospital with my sister, and we had to wait for visiting hours to begin. Her husband, Herbert, came in and sat down across from us.

What I did not know was that Herbert had glaucoma and had lost his sight. He couldn't see anything.

I was talking to Dick (Richard), and after a few minutes, Herbert said, "Geraldine, is that you?" I said,

"Yes, and as pretty as I ever was, not one wrinkle and still blonde." He started laughing, and so did everyone else in the room.

Then we all went upstairs to see Bootsy. She had lost a lot of weight, and her complexion was yellow. They had done exploratory surgery, closed her up after doing an external bowel resection, and were giving her morphine for the intense pain. You could tell she was in pain; she could hardly smile.

We went every day to see her. When I told my boss about her he told me I could take all the time off I needed. To add to her pain, someone from housekeeping came in one day to clean the room.

When she went behind the bed, she knocked the cord out of the socket of the machine that was being used to help Bootsy. Of course it was an accident, but Bootsy started going into convulsions before someone noticed the light was out on the machine, and called for the nurse.

I was furious! I told them, "Don't let her come in here, again!"

Bootsy could hardly speak above a whisper, and it was hard for her to talk to me. I would sit beside her bed, real close, and talk to her. I told her the whole thing was like a nightmare, and she agreed.

One day I had on a dress that she liked a lot. She wanted one just like it to wear on Thanksgiving. I told her we'd all be together. I told Dick about it on the way home. I said,

"She must be getting better. She's talking about going home." He said, "No, she's not, Gerry. People with cancer do that. They think they are getting better." Maybe it was the morphine. The doctor had left orders that anytime she wanted it, she could have it.

She also asked Dick if he would take Herbert to Rochester to get trained with a leader dog for the blind. After she died, we did just that. Herbert got a beautiful, large Golden Shepherd, named Anoka, who loved him and stayed with him until he died.

On December 20, 1971, we had gone home to change clothes, bathe, and rest some. While we were gone, Bootsy died. We were spared having to be there when she died. My only regret was that we hadn't stayed close.

I remembered the times we had gone to church together. There was one song we used to sing. Every night, while we stayed with her, I could hear the song in my head. It was called, "The Promised Land." The words to the chorus kept ringing in my ears,

"I am bound for the Promised Land,
O who will come and go with me?
I am bound for the Promised Land."

Bootsy's girls, Vicky was about 14, and Terry was either 12 or 13 when she died. A few years later, Herbert died of cancer, leaving the girls with neither parent. Vicky passed away in 2001, leaving only Terry, and we have lost touch with her.

Chapter Forty Two
Dedicated to Bootsy and Herbert

Beatrice Lorine Oxford – Winchell
Born May 1, 1926 – Died December 20, 1971

I have to tell of my sister Beatrice's love and loyalty.

When I came home from California, I was just in the first month of my pregnancy with Chuck. I don't know how long I had been home, but Bootsy and I had gone somewhere. Walking home, we met this couple. When they passed, we all spoke to one another.

The man was tall and good looking, with black hair. He smiled at me, as big as he could. When we were past them, Bootsy said he was just doing that to make his wife mad because she was a jealous person, and he was well known for chasing women.

That evening he came to the house and asked to speak with me. We were all very surprised, and everyone was looking out the window, listening and watching to see just what he wanted with me.

He said he wanted to know how I was, and how Clarence got the nickname, "Motor?"

I told him I was going to have a baby, and that Clarence was out in Idaho. Seems he knew Clarence from playing pool and cards with him. That was it. Then he left.

Later, I left to go to Idaho to be with Clarence when I had Chuck. After I came back, my mother told me that his wife had come to the house looking for me. He had apparently told her he had gone out with me. They had no idea I wasn't even there. Bootsy had told her that her husband was a liar, and that I had been gone for months.

She insisted that I had been going out with her husband, and Bootsy just hauled off and hit her. My mother said they fought all over the front yard and into the rose bushes. Bootsy was scratched all over, but she wouldn't give up and finally the wife left, crying.

When we lived at the Fort Clark Apartments, Bootsy and I would stop at the little market on the way home from work. The men who ran the store were friendly, and she would always laugh and talk to them. One day they asked her why I didn't talk to them.

She told them I was afraid to because my husband was the jealous type. They told her jealously is all right if it's a little, but too much was like spice, it could ruin things.

One of the ladies I worked with invited me to her wedding shower. I really wanted to go but I was afraid to even suggest it to Clarence. I told Bootsy about it. Another girl I worked with was going to drive and had offered to come and pick me up, take me there and bring me home. Bootsy said for me just to get dressed and go.

She said, "Clarence can't stop you." I tell you what, it took some nerve, but I did it.

And, Bootsy was right; Clarence didn't say a word about it.

Bootsy was pretty and kind. Her husband, Herbert Winchell, was one of the kindest men to ever walk upon the face of this earth. But their lives were, what I call, a tragedy. They took Jim and Cat, who were 15 and 10, into their home to save them from our father, after our mother passed away. Our father wouldn't try to keep a home for his children. In fact, he even moved in with Bootsy and Herbert for a while, and terrorized them in their own home with his drunken brawls.

Bootsy had been married at least eleven or twelve years before she became pregnant with their eldest daughter, Vicky Lynn. During this pregnancy, her doctor gave her a drug called Diethylstilbestrol, or DES, to reduce her chances of a miscarriage. I believe it later caused her cancer, and eventually her death, because there is no history of cancer in our family.

When Vicky was a young woman, she had a cancerous tumor removed. Many years later, doctors found a link between mothers and daughters of patients who took DES. Vicky eventually was diagnosed with Lupus, and died due to complications at the young age of 44.

Bootsy did not take DES during her second pregnancy with their second daughter, Terry Lynn.

Not only did Bootsy have to deal with her cancer, and eventually lose her life to it, but she also had to watch Herbert lose his sight to glaucoma. A real-life tragedy!

Chapter Forty-Three
Dedicated to Gloria Ann, "Cat"

Gloria Ann Oxford – Stajda
Born January 26, 1934 - Died November 29, 1980

It was the day I received the phone call. The phone rang, and on the other end a voice said, "Aunt Gerry, our mother has killed herself."

Now there is a nightmare! You don't want to believe this is actually happening. My first thought was of the two little girls, Mary Ann and Connie, her son Gregory, and husband Mack. How awful this must be for them!

When we arrived at Cat and Mack's house, the two girls were sitting in the middle of the living room floor, rocking in silence. They were both in serious shock. Mack, who was much older than Cat, was drinking a beer and talking in confusion.

Apparently Cat was afraid of the neighborhood that they lived in. We all knew she kept a baseball bat behind the door, but what we didn't know was that she had started sleeping with a loaded gun under her pillow. Mack had begged her not to keep it there, because it had a hairpin trigger.

During the night, sound asleep; she must have moved wrong and the gun fired, striking her in the head. My baby sister, Gloria Ann, the one I named "Kathleen" and called "Cat" was dead at the age of 46.

During earlier years, Clarence and I would go over to visit. We would all drink beer, staying for a good long time, laughing and singing the old southern songs. She liked the songs: "Rocky Top," "That Good Old' Mountain Dew," "Jeremiah Was a Bullfrog" and "Fraulein," by Bobby Helms. I never could understand why she liked "Fraulein." Now I have a CD of it, and it's just a pretty love song. After I quit drinking, I wasn't any fun for her to be with.

She loved to hunt mushrooms in the early morning dew. Every year she planted Silver Dollar flowers in the small back yard she had. There were always desserts in the freezer for the children.

She was famous for her goulash. She had a wall in her pantry hanging with every size cast iron cooking utensil ever made.

Her house was always immaculate, and her children were always dressed nice and well groomed.

She loved her children. She also liked to play Michigan Rummy, and often she tried to teach me how to play it, too.

One time when our father was still alive, she went down to Kentucky and brought him back to River Rouge, where she lived. He was old, and not getting around very well.

We had a family reunion at her house. Magdalene and Elmer, Bootsy and Herbert, Clarence and I were all there with all of our children, and we took family photos. It was a potluck, and the food was fantastic!

She told her two girls how hard it had been for her as a child, that her mother was sick and her father a drunk. It was the truth and we loved her.

She did tell me she liked the song, "Just a Rose Will Do." We had a trio from our church, Lakeside Missionary Baptist in Newport; sing it for us at her funeral service.

In May of 1986, Mack died of a heart attack. The nice looking man who in 1962, had come and told Bootsy and I that he was the proud father of a beautiful baby girl, Mary Ann, was gone to us all.

Epilogue
(The Rest of My Story)

After I wrote these stories, I thought I was done.

But I got a phone call from Sharon saying, "Mother, you are not done yet. You have to tell the rest of your story."

I asked her, "What do you want me to write?"

She answered, "Start with when you married Dick."

So, here is the REST of my story, written on February 15, 2005.

My life really changed after I met and married Richard (Dick) Ponto on January 17, 1969. When we first met I was a sales clerk for a men's clothing department of a retail store, and he was the department manager.

Sometime after that, Dick went to work for another department store, called Federals as the Store Manager, some time later it went out of business. Then he went to work at Ford Motor Co., in Flat Rock. I went to work for another Ford Motor Co. Plant in Monroe. Between the two of us, we started making good money, more than either one of us had ever made. We had great benefits, paid vacations, and great healthcare coverage.

We were living in that two-bedroom house in Newport, with a living room, kitchen and one and a-half baths. We owned the house, but after discussion, we decided to sell it and build a new one.

In 1974 we had a new home built. It was a beautiful house. It had three bedrooms, two full baths upstairs and a half bath on the main floor, a kitchen with a separate eating area, a formal dining room, a family room, a formal living room, a full basement, a redwood deck and a two-car garage. We furnished it with all new Ethan Allen furniture, new custom-made curtains and drapes that were hung by professionals. We both had new cars, and life was the best it had ever been for both of us. We had a house-warming party with family and friends. Sharon came with Ronnie and Bobbi Jo, two of my grandchildren.

While we lived there, my brother Jim lived in Curacao, Netherlands Antilles in the Dutch West Indies. He sent airplane tickets for my sister and me to visit him. He warned us to get a suntan before we came. When he came out of the Air Force he went to work for ALM & LKM Airlines as a Technical Director, in the maintenance and engineering department, and moved up in the ranks, until they sent him there to open the airport for them.

Dick drove us from Michigan to Kennedy Airport in New York to use the tickets. We got to see New York City. Dick had been there while he was in the Navy. He took us to see the Statue of Liberty. I climbed halfway up and waved down at my sister and him. We saw Ellis Island, too. I had never seen so many bridges in one place. And, Chinatown! What a sight!

Curacao was beautiful. Tropical birds, trees, flowers, white sandy beaches, clean blue water, and hotels with gambling and so many different foods that I wasn't used to. There were also big cemeteries where people were buried on top of the ground. I had never seen that before. The music of the steel bands was great, and the open markets with no flies; the trees leaned all in one direction from the hard winds blowing all the time. We were there for two weeks.

When it came time for us to come home, Dick drove, again, from Michigan to New York to pick us up. I sure had missed him, and he was happy to see me, too. We were happy to be home. I found out one thing from that trip. The beautiful green mountains of the "good old USA" can't be beat. It truly is "Home, Sweet Home."

The years we lived in our new home were nice. My first granddaughter, Theresa Kay, would come out and spend time with us. She was born May 26, 1969, the year Dick and I got married. So she would have been about 5 or 6 then. She spent one Easter with us.

I remember putting her up on the counter of the sink, and coloring Easter Eggs together. When she was in the first grade, all the little crafts she made in school were for her grandma.

I still have them in a shoebox. I showed them to her a few years ago, and she looked at me and laughed.

She said, "Grandma's are silly."

In May of 1977, we had a falling out with the builder, sold the house, and moved back to our old house in Newport. We had all the new furniture, and Sharon had come with her children, Ronnie and Bobbie Jo, to live with us. The house was too small, so we decided to remodel it.

We ended up with another two-story home. It had four bedrooms, another very large living room, dining room, new kitchen, and new bathroom. Shortly after that, Sharon got remarried and moved with her children to Homestead, Florida.

I sure hated to see her go. I loved my grandchildren. I used to put them up on the kitchen counter and watch their happy, little faces while I cut up pumpkins for Jack-O-Lanterns.

We had birthday parties, watched them go to school on their first day, and took them to have their pictures taken with Santa Claus. Dick and I even took Bobbie Jo with us on our second trip to Niagara Falls.

Those years that Sharon lived with us were good for her. She had married so young, she was only 16 and had children right away, and coming home gave her some time to be a young woman. She loved to dance, and met a young man who loved to dance.

They won a lot of Disco dance contests together.

Well, life doesn't stop just because your children leave home. The plant that Dick worked in shut down in 1981. He was trying to get another job when Ford offered the laid-off workers jobs in Ohio or Missouri. Dick chose to go to Missouri, and he left in September of 1982. He came home almost every weekend. Meanwhile, I am living alone for the first time in my life.

I asked my son, John, to bring his family and live with me.

I worked until June of 1983, when I retired from Ford, and moved to St. Louis, Missouri, to be with Dick. We had a nice apartment there. Bobbie Jo and Ronnie came when school was out to spend the summer with us. There were tennis courts and a swimming pool in the apartment complex. After their visit, they flew home to Florida. Theresa came and visited us, too.

We lived in the apartment for a year. Then we built another house in O'Fallon, Missouri. It was a nice three-bedroom, two-bath home; and everything was new again. We loved this house.

Dick worked afternoons. After he would leave, I would plant flowers in the yard. One fall, I planted seven hundred tulips. I spent many happy hours in the yard. It was the first time in my life I could do something I really wanted to do. I gave my rock garden a name, "My Jewel Box." It was pretty, and I had rocks from just every place I had traveled to.

In 1986, Sharon brought her children and came to Missouri. She got a home of her own, out in the country. It was quite a culture shock for her children, coming from Miami to the country in Missouri. So, for a while her children lived with us in the city.

Sharon helped me with my flower garden. She gave me all kinds of plants, and she worked on one for herself at her house. She ended up with eleven flower gardens, all in different places on her six acres of land. She had a vegetable garden, she canned, and she helped me wallpaper my entire house. Some of the designs on the wallpaper were floral. She pointed out that I was nostalgic about the paper.

In May of 1992, I talked her into taking me to Kentucky to decorate my mother's grave. I wanted her to know where her grandmother was buried. My brother, Jim, came over from Virginia, where he now lives, and met us there. We had a nice visit.

Sharon said, "Mother, if we hurry, we can get home in time to see Ronnie graduate from high school." Ronnie graduated on May 24th.

I had time on my hands, so I decided to get an education. A teacher lived a few houses from me. I asked her if she would teach me, to tutor me. Her name was Torrie Sanders. She tutored me from November of 1991 to February of 1992. Then she told me that she had taught me all she could, and I needed to go over to the high school to take the GED classes. She explained all about them.

In 1992, Bobbie Jo quit high school. Sharon enrolled her in the GED classes because, one way or another, she was determined Bobbie Jo would get an education. It was the perfect time for me to attend those classes, too.

When we started the classes, Bobbie Jo came to live with us. It was fun having her there. The boys in the classes flirted with her. She would get up to take a break, and the boys would get up, too. I'd raise my finger and motion for them to sit back down. They would look at one another.

The ones that knew would tell the others, "It's her grandmother." And, soon they didn't pay any attention to me.

One of our teachers, Floyd Colbert, talked to me. He knew how little knowledge I had. He told me how hard it was going to be. I told him I wouldn't quit. Dick hired a tutor to help me with mathematics, named Fran Hagman, who came to the house once or twice a week. That helped.

Life was good.

John and his family came to see us with his wife, Heather, and their children Jessie, Ruth, Michelle and Max, my grandchildren.

Chuck surprised me one Mother's Day. We went to Sharon's for dinner, and everything was decorated nicely. She was in the kitchen, cooking and setting the table for dinner. Everyone else was in the living room, watching TV and acting normal.

After a few minutes, I heard, "Who said you could come out here?"

There he was, coming out of one of the bedrooms. Chuck, my first-born, laughing and smiling at my surprise, I just screamed.

The night before Sharon had gone to the airport to pick him up. She took him out to her house without telling Dick or me. Everyone was laughing at my overwhelmed surprise. It was one of the nicest Mother's Days I have ever had.

One year, we went to Estes Park in Colorado for a vacation. Another time we went to California to visit one of Dick's sisters and one of my cousins. On the way there, we went to the Grand Canyon, and on the way back, we visited it again. While in the Mohave Desert, I made Dick stop so I could pick up rocks.

He kept telling me, "You can't do that." There wasn't a person within sight, for miles.

"Who is going to see me?" I asked him.

I had rocks in my flower garden from every state we had been in.

I'm not the only rock hound in my family. There are a few of us: my daughter, for one, and a couple of my nieces, Mary Ann and Debbie. And, they love flowers as much as I do.

While we lived in Missouri, we went to visit the Arch, in St. Louis, many times. When we had visitors in from out of town we would always take them downtown to see it.

Dick started having pain in both his knees. He ended up having surgery to rebuild and replace them, and was unable to work at his job. He eventually retired in 1992. In the winter it would snow and be cold, and he would go out and shovel snow. I was always afraid he would fall. In 1993 I convinced him we should move to Florida, for a good life in the "sunshine state." We sold the house and Bobbie Jo moved back to her mother's.

We moved to Palm Bay, FL, where we found a beautiful house. It had three bedrooms and two baths, a formal dining room, living room, kitchen with a breakfast room, family room, two-car garage, an enclosed in-ground swimming pool, and a cedar-fenced back yard. When we moved, Sharon and Bobbie Jo came down and helped us unpack and set up the house. Sharon also did some stenciling work in the kitchen.

Bobbie Jo stayed and we redecorated the house. I didn't like the colors that were on the walls, so we painted all of them. We also got new carpeting and white tile for the floors. Thank God the pool was screened in because the lizards and snakes were just awful there!

The first contact I had with the lizards was at the nursery, when I was looking for plants. I was so happy with all the new, pretty, tropical plants. Then a lizard ran across the floor. I yelled, and everyone looked at me like, "What is the matter with you?"

They were so bad, I had Dick buy the spray you kill hornets with, and I would spray them when they got on the screens around the pool.

Then there were the snakes. They were in the yard and in the gardens; one of them even got into the house. I killed it with a butcher knife. (Old habits are hard to break.) I had gotten up in the middle of the night to use the bathroom. There it was, by the sink. I sprayed it with hair spray, to blind it, went into the kitchen and got the biggest knife I owned. I went back into the bathroom and chopped it into little pieces. After the head was chopped off, it still was trying to bite me.

Dick came into the bathroom, half a-sleep, and said, "What is going on?"

I said, "Look!"

There it lay, chopped up into little pieces, with blood all over the floor. He was in shock. It wasn't really a very big snake, about two feet long. But, to me it was big enough!

One year, Sharon came down and we went down to Key West together. That is the "true" Florida. Everything down there is beautiful. She bought tickets for us to sail on a sunset cruise on a 78' ship that a friend of hers had built. It looked like something the Pilgrims had come over on, big and black. She told me it was a replica of a two mast, square topsail English Clipper, and that it was seventy-eight feet long. It started to rain before we could get on it, and she got a refund on the tickets.

We window-shopped for tee shirts and stopped to have a few drinks along the way at some of the outdoor cafes. We went into one shell shop. It was full of shells, and it was so pretty that you could spend all day just looking.

We went to a pastry shop and got coffee and guava pastries that Sharon missed, from when she lived in Florida before. We walked along the street, eating the pastries and drinking our coffee. We passed a couple of men, didn't pay any attention to them, and got into the car.

All of a sudden we heard police sirens. Mind you, we were still drinking our coffee and eating pastries. A police car pulled right up in front of our car, blocking us, and another one pulled up behind us. An officer jumped out of his car, ran up on the sidewalk, pulled his gun out and pointed it at us.

After one look at our amazed looks, the coffee and pastries, it was obvious we had nothing to do with what was going on. Another officer had his gun drawn, too, and they cuffed and arrested the two men we had passed. One of the men had a white bag, taped to himself under his shirt. We realized we were in the middle of a cocaine drug bust.

The officers motioned for us to go, which we didn't hesitate about doing. Because of the rain and wind we couldn't really do anything else, so we just decided to go on home. Never in your wildest imagination would you think this could happen to you. Brings home the phrase of being in the wrong place at the wrong time, doesn't it?

Now I am still going to school, and I really enjoy it. The young people are fun to be around, and they laugh at me. One day I shined up a big, red apple and took it to the teacher. He laughed, too.

In 1994, Bobbie Jo came back to Florida, and we both took the tests for our GED. Now both of us have our High School Diplomas. I did well on my scores, even if I did have to take the math test twice. The stuff on the math test I had just learned, and it was hard. I am now 71 years old.

You are never too old to get an education. I always took that to heart. It gave me the courage to do it. I would like to say, "If I can do it, anyone can do it." I am living, walking proof of it.

By now, we are both tired of living in Florida. We want to go back to Michigan, to where we both call "home." Dick says we cannot go until we build up some equity in the Palm Bay house.

I say, "Okay, but will you take me to Kentucky? I want to visit my mother's grave, again." We went to Jenkins, and I went up to Dunham where I grew up. I walked around, and visited and talked with people. Everybody was a stranger to me, except for two people. One of them was the woman who lived in the last house that we lived in when we were there.

The house was bigger than I remembered it to be. I wonder why it seemed smaller when we lived there. Then I remember. It's because there were six of us children and our mother and father were all living there. No wonder it seemed small.

Mrs. Arnett, the woman who now lived in the house, offered to have us spend the night. We thanked her, but told her we couldn't because we had our two dogs with us.

Then we went to Millstone, where my mother grew up. We visited the boarding house where she worked and met our father at, and the house she lived in on Broad Branch with her Aunt and Uncle Mayo Holbrook. The lady who lived in the house then, told me one of my cousins always comes back on Memorial Day, to decorate his parents' graves, and he would come there and walk through the whole house. She wanted to know if I wanted to do that, too. I said I was okay just visiting with her. The barn we played in, as children, was still there.

In 1998, I thanked God to be leaving Florida and going back to Michigan. We stored all our furnishings in Chuck's garage, and once again started looking for a house. We found it, up north in Oscoda. It's not a big, beautiful house, but it's a nice house, with two acres of land and all kinds of trees in a wooded area.

The house has the one thing I love about a house; the bedrooms are all upstairs. It's what they call a split-level home.

I have my rock gardens back, (with no snakes). We have a vegetable garden, again. Dick has a 2000 truck, a riding lawn mower, a tiller, and other "boy toys." The truck is blue, and I love riding in it. Often we have family that comes to visit, and we go to visit them.

As of 2003, Sharon lives in Castle Rock, Colorado, with her husband, Jim. Dick and I went to visit them. We also saw the grandkids, Ronnie and Bobbie Jo, in St. Louis, along with my great-grandchildren. Then we took a trip to Bar Harbor, Maine and took a ferry to Nova Scotia, Canada.

I was telling Dick, at the breakfast table one morning, "You know, the house is painted and papered, the yard is landscaped nicely. It must be time for us to move again."

He laughed and said, "No way!"

Since I have come back to Michigan, one of Cat's girls, Connie, called me and asked me to go visit her. While I was there she asked what I would like to do. I had been watching line dancing on TV, and knowing the girls liked to dance, I told her, "I'd like to go line dancing."

She laughed and said, "I'll find out where we can go."

She got together with her lady friends, and two of them said they would go with us. Her sister, Mary Ann, said she wanted to go, too.

They found a place, called The Diamond Back. When we got there, the place looked familiar. Then I remembered; this was the place where Sharon used to go to Disco dancing. The place now looks like the one Toby Keith sings about in "I Love this Bar." They taught line dancing for an hour, and then they taught the Texas Two-step. We stayed till we were tired out. While we were there, we called Chuck to come over and dance with us.

He said, "Mother, I can't. They threw me out of there."

I had a great time. I got to do something I had wanted to do ever since I first saw it on TV.

After writing about my life using a yellow legal ad and pencil, there are still a few things I would like to add.

That all three of my children grew up healthy and that I am proud of them, each in their own accomplishments and courage. Out of my marriage to their father they were a blessing to me.

I did the best I could raising them, I loved all three of them, even though my daughter says, I loved the first born more, but that is impossible, as I have always loved my children equally.

My grandchildren I have brought me much comfort and adoration, Chucky, Theresa, Ronnie, Bobbi Jo, Jessie, Ruth, Michelle and Max. They are brilliant young individuals, whom all have grown into fine upstanding adults with children of their own. I want to tell them that I am proud of them also and thank you for being a constant part of my life. It has brought me many warm and comforting memories when I sit and think back.

The great grandchildren - Joshua, Jacob, Ethan, Brian, Marcus, Tasia Jo, Gabrielle, Ronnie, Austin, Ava, Gary and Miles it has been a true honor to see them come into this world and see how proud their parents and grandparents are of them.

My life has been rich and good, I truly love you all.

Editor's Note

Although it has been a lengthy process, what an extraordinary privilege it has been to help you tell the story of your mesmerizing life.

So many magnificent things I have learned about you. So proud of you for the strength, courage and the endurance you have shown, and grateful to be your daughter.

You are a very beautiful and strong woman, which I admire and cherish the most. What wonderful memories you have! What a life! What a legacy to leave for others!

In spite of the hardships you endured, the difficult path you had to walk, and life's hard lessons, your amazing spirit still shines through today. You are filled with laughter, generosity, abundant kindness and are wonderful to keep company with. You were always a loving mother, when our own father would not provide, you found a way to make things happen. We are and will be eternally grateful for all the sacrifices you made for your children. Thank you for being my mentor, my best friend, and my role model.

Dick was so right when he said, "Tell it like it was."

Thank you, mother, for trusting me to share in telling your story!

"I Love You & Happy 85th Birthday Mother"

Sharon Kay
May 6, 2008

Four Maternal Generations
1998
Geraldine Ponto, Sharon Harris, Bobbi Jo Smith & Tasia Jo Gonz

Chapter Forty Four
The Tolliver Vendetta

Geraldine Tolliver-Oxford-Ponto states that this is about our "Tolliver" family members and that they were from Rowan Co, Kentucky.

THE TOLLIVER-MARTIN-LOGAN VENDETTA Reprinted from Kentucky's Famous Feuds and Tragedies by Charles G. Mutzenber, 1917, R.F. Fenno & Co., New York

The royal murder at Sarajevo was the spark that set the world on fire. It would be silly, however, to place the blame of the world war upon it. To find the real causes of the appalling tragedy one must go further back.

So it is with the great Rowan County war. There were many agencies at work that contributed, little by little, but nonetheless surely, to that state of anarchy, which disgraced Rowan County and Kentucky during the eighties. The evil influences, which initiated it, were: Politics and Whiskey. A weak kneed, yea, corrupt administration of justice permitted its continuation. The reign of terror, which continued so long unhindered, could have been crushed in its infancy with any sort of an honest, determined effort at law enforcement.

A verse or two of Mulligan's "in Kentucky" finds excellent application here:

"The bluegrass waves the bluest In Kentucky;
Yet, bluebloods are the fewest (?) In Kentucky;
Moonshine is the clearest, by no means the dearest,
And yet, it acts the queerest In Kentucky.
"The dove-notes are the saddest, In Kentucky:
The streams dance on the gladdest In Kentucky:
Hip pockets are the thickest, Pistol hands the slickest,
The cylinder turns quickest In Kentucky.
"The song birds are the sweetest In Kentucky:

The thoroughbreds are fleetest In Kentucky:

Mountains tower proudest, Thunder peals the loudest the landscape is the grandest, AND POLITICS - the worse In Kentucky."

In the long continued struggle which brought Rowan County into disrepute, many families of high reputation, men of wealth and influence, as well as men of reckless, undaunted, desperate character, were pitted against each other.

Officers of the law, lawyers, judges and politicians of more than ordinary ability and reputation, quarreled, disputed and excited such unreasoning passion as to result in bloodshed. After that the dogged, stubborn determination of the different factions admitted of no other settlement of the controversy save by the arbitrate of arms, a war to the death. Patrick Henry cried out before the Virginia Convention: "Gentlemen may cry peace, peace, but there is no peace."

In Rowan County, too, men cried continually for peace, yet there was to be no peace until anarchy had almost depopulated the county and its name had become synonymous with outlawry. The only alternative left was to leave the country or fight. Some did leave; most of them remained and fought, fought with courage worthy of a better cause. The courts appeared powerless. The officers were themselves bitter partisans.

The government of the State, when applied to for troops to assist in restoring order, sometimes refused aid, owing to a technicality in the law, and thus was precipitated the famous bloody battle at Morehead, in which many men were killed and wounded. It may be well to add that Rowan County was not a remote, inaccessible region where civilization had made but little progress, as was the case along the border of West Virginia and Kentucky, the scene of the Hatfield-McCoy war.

Good roads and railroad communication had introduced to Rowan County even then a civilization, which should have made the bloody conflict impossible; it certainly made it inexcusable.

It is difficult to produce a fair picture of the political upheavals and complications, which eventually led to and resulted in so much bloodshed without going behind the actual outbreak of the feud. While this necessitates the narration of incidents of purely local interest, and may, therefore, not grip the interest of outsiders, a patient reading of it will develop the fact that it is indispensable to a true understanding of the history of this war, and also that it teaches a moral.

As early as 1874 political quarrels arose engendering bitter hatred, between prominent, wealthy and influential men of Rowan and surrounding counties. At that time it was hoped and generally believed that the difficulties would be forgotten as soon as the heat of the political contests had abated. But as the years passed factional division grew more and more pronounced.

Citizens, who had theretofore held aloof from the disputes, were gradually and surely drawn into the vortex of strife. As is usual and unavoidable under such circumstances, many desperate, degraded characters attached themselves to the various factions.

These would commit deeds for pay, from the commission of which the more circumspect employers of them shrank in fear. In such wars the hired assassin always finds lucrative employment. He becomes the blind tool of the coward with the money, and the greater the compensation the more horrible his crimes. The innocent but direct cause of the political struggle to which we must refer, was the Honorable Thomas F. Hargis, who, in after years, rose to the highest judicial position in the state. His father, before him, served in the constitutional convention of the State in 1849 and was a very distinguished Kentuckian.

When the great rebellion broke out, Kentucky soon began to suffer the distress and horrors of civil war. It at first declared its intention to remain neutral. Governor McGoffin refused to furnish troops to the Union army and attempted to enforce neutrality by maintaining a "Home Guard." This brought on many conflicts with the State Guards. It became at once apparent that the two bodies of troops were nothing more than partisans. The Home Guards often employed their military power and authority in harassing and mistreating actual or suspected sympathizers with the cause of the South.

The State Guards, on the other hand, used their influence and made every exertion toward turning the tide of public sentiment in favor of the Confederacy. The sudden invasion of Kentucky by the federal troops was greeted with joy by the Home Guards, who made no attempt to repel it or so preserve the State's neutrality for which purpose they had been organized.

The larger portion of the Home Guards, in fact, at once joined the Union army. The State Guards disbanded and a majority of them joined the Confederates. The division of Kentucky was now complete. In the general rush to opposing armies we find Thomas Hargis donning the gray and fighting for the "Lost Cause" as captain until the close of the war. Returning home, he studied law and was admitted to the bar. The date of this admission, an unimportant point it may seem, was nevertheless responsible for the internecine strife of after years.

In the year 1874, Captain Hargis, who had already won prominence as a lawyer of ability and sagacity, was nominated by the Democratic Party as its candidate for judge of the circuit court. Opposed to Hargis in this race was Geo. M. Thomas, afterwards United States District Attorney for the District of Kentucky. He was the nominee of the Republican Party.

The race was exceedingly hot and spirited from the beginning. The contest became bitter. It was charged by the friends of Thomas, among whom were not only the Republicans whose nominee and choice he was, but enemies of Hargis in the ranks of his own party, that he was not eligible to the office because he had not attained the requisite age, and that he was still further disqualified from holding the position of Circuit Judge because he had not been licensed as a lawyer for a sufficient number of years. These reports were industriously circulated against him.

Appreciating the danger of such a rumor in a contest like this was, and knowing that only a prompt refutation and repudiation of the charges could prevent his signal and disastrous defeat, he hastened to obtain copies of the records of his age, and of the date of his admission to the bar from the records of the Clerk's office. At the time of his candidacy Hargis was a resident of Carlisle, Nicholas County, but when admitted to the practice of the law had resided in Rowan County. So the records of his admission to the bar must be obtained there. He, therefore, went at once to Morehead and instituted an examination of the records, but to his consternation it revealed the astounding fact that the only record and evidence of his admission to the bar had been mutilated and destroyed; the pages containing them had been cut out from the books.

Added to this was the unwelcome discovery that the family Bible had also been mutilated in so far as it contained the record of his age. The charges of ineligibility had been widely circulated and published in the newspapers and Hargis' inability to refute them for lack of record evidence now gave them the stamp and color of truth. The Republicans, and the personal enemies of Hargis among the Democrats, were jubilant, while his friends flatly and broadly accused Thomas' friends and supporters of the crime of stealing and destroying public records.

This further increased the already bitter feeling. The friends of Thomas now charged that if any such records had ever existed Hargis himself had stolen and destroyed them. The result of it all was that Hargis was defeated by his Republican opponent, and this in a district theretofore always safely Democratic. The close of the contest brought out another truth no longer to be denied or over looked. Every circumstance and condition existing after the election pointed clearly to the fact that something more than factional, political animosity, common in all hotly contested races for position, had been awakened and that in the hearts of many, malice had taken deep root. Each succeeding election only augmented the bitter feeling.

Desire for revenge, and, what at first seemed but political excitement and zeal for the favored candidate, now caused friends of old to cancel their friendship and the most prominent leaders of the opposing factions regarded each other no longer as merely political, but as personal enemies.

In the year 1876 the Legislature of Kentucky created a Circuit Court for Commonwealth proceedings alone, the new district being composed of the same counties as the old. Hargis again announced himself a candidate for judge of the newly organized court. This time he was elected with an easy majority. He continued in this office, which he filled with signal ability, until in the spring of 1879, when an event took place, which opened to him the road to still higher honors, and also still further fanned the flame of political and personal strife.

The event referred to the vacancy created on the bench of the Court of Appeals as the result of a tragedy enacted upon the streets of the state, at Frankfort, the assassination of Appellate Judge J.M. Elliott, by one Thomas Buford. The tragic death of this able jurist horrified all Kentucky. His slayer pleaded insanity. The trial jury on first ballot stood six for conviction and six for acquittal on the ground of insanity. Finally, the verdict of the whole jury declared him insane. He was transferred to the Asylum at Anchorage where he remained but a short time. He escaped to Indiana where he remained because our requisition laws were then not sufficient to enforce his return to Kentucky.

Immediately after the death of Justice Elliott an election was ordered for his successor and Judge Hargis again became a candidate before the Democratic convention. A number of able and distinguished jurists opposed him before that body, many of these much older and experienced than he. In spite of the powerful opposition brought to bear against him, Judge Hargis again succeeded in obtaining the nomination, another proof of his political influence as well as of his talents as a lawyer and politician.

This last and most important success of Hargis aroused anew the malign hatred and envy of his numerous enemies in the camps of his own party. The old charges were renewed, remodeled, rehashed, renovated and added to, as the occasion demanded. The story of his willful, felonious destruction and mutilation of court records was republished and more extensively circulated than ever.

Newspapers, circulars, handbills and letters telling the story were scattered throughout the district, posted up at all public places, on fences and trees along the highways, thus increasing factional enmity to a dangerous intensity. Opposed to him in this race was Judge Holt, a Republican politician and lawyer of prominence, and of unassailable purity of character. The contest between these men was waged with spirit with the result that the mantle of Judge Elliott fell upon Judge Hargis. During the canvass Judge Hargis, through the Courier Journal and other newspapers, had denounced the person over whose signatures a number of scandalous accusations and derogatory charges had been made, as liars, calumniators and villains.

Thomas M. Green, editor of the Maysville Eagle, also correspondent of the Cincinnati Commercial Gazette, had been persistent in industriously keeping the disparaging accusations against Hargis in the columns of the Republican press of the country. Hargis in consequence, singled out Editor

Green in his card to the Courier Journal as the chief offender, assailing him in most bitter terms. Green applied to the law for redress and instituted suit for libel in the Jefferson Circuit Court at Louisville, asking for a large sum in damages.

Early in the spring of 1880 the case came on for trial. Hargis waived all questions of jurisdiction, which it had been expected he would use as a defense. He somewhat staggered his enemies by admitting responsibility for the article upon which the suit was based, and declaring his ability to prove the charges made against Green as true. The trial lasted for many months. It was minutely reported in the press of the country and read everywhere. Even now the angel of good fortune did not desert Judge Hargis. He won the case.

During this period, the controversy between Green and Hargis had very sharply aligned the friends and enemies of Rowan County. So complete was the breach that the thoughtful ones looked forward to open, actual hostilities. Hope of compromise disappeared as time passed. A storm so long brewing is apt to accumulate extraordinary force. A fury long pent up will break loose with greater fierceness. The strife had penetrated every neighborhood, almost every household. Any public occasion, especially the biennial election, was looked forward to with dread. Minor politician contests, waged in these elections, served to open old sores and to inflict new wounds, adding material for the spirit of revenge to feed upon.

At that time the Australian ballot system had not yet been introduced. The viva voce system was in vogue, and bribery in elections was, therefore, much more common than it is now. Candidates practically bought their offices. The voter cast his vote publicly; it was recorded publicly, and cried out publicly.

In this wise the buyer of the vote controlled the seller, and, very often, vote sellers were driven en masse to the polls so many sheep, a cause of innumerable election fights. Another successful instigator of trouble on Election Day was the free and promiscuous use of liquor with which candidates treated and influenced the voters. Election contests frequently excite the most staid and conservative citizens, but when whiskey is added it is certain to arouse passions, which might, other wise, have slumbered on.

Such were conditions in Rowan County on the day of election, August 1884. A hot political race was on between one S.B. Goodan, the Democratic nominee for sheriff of the county, and W.C. Humphrey, commonly known as Cook Humphrey, the Republican nominee. The county being almost equally divided politically, the contest was close. Each of the candidates was wealthy, influential and extensively related. Money was used without stint; bar rooms were thrown wide open at Morehead, the county seat, and principal town of the county, as well as at most other precincts in the county.

The town was crowded with excited, angry, drunken men and all through the day there were fist fights and brawls. During one of these, the prelude to the conflict, which afterward attracted the attention of the American press, John Martin, son of Ben Martin, a wealthy farmer, was struck down and seriously injured. He immediately sprang to his feet, drew his pistol and a general pistol battle followed. When the smoke had cleared away, Solomon Bradley was found dead, and Adam Sizemore severely wounded. The death of Bradley, a good citizen, who had taken no part in the fighting, and the wounding of Sizemore and Martin proved of fatal consequences.

Bradley was one of the most influential Republicans of the county. He and John Martin were members of the best families and extensively related even in adjoining counties. The Martins were known to be ambitious and brave men. It appeared that Martin received his wounds at the hands of Floyd Tolliver, a brother of Craig Tolliver, who afterwards attained such unenviable notoriety and bore the distinction of being one of the most cruel, blood thirsty desperadoes Kentucky ever had the misfortune to own as her son, and whose tragic death on the memorable battle at Morehead some years later was heralded throughout the country. John C. Day, the then acting Sheriff of Rowan County, was charged with the shooting and wounding of Sizemore. The first blood had now been spilt; more was bound to follow.

Even the most hopeful became convinced that a long and bloody conflict could no longer be averted. Those best acquainted with the state of affairs knew, and rightly predicted, that the law would not be invoked to settle the trouble and punish the offenders. "A life for a life" was the motto that henceforth governed the factions, now arrayed against each other in open, desperate warfare.

The wounding of Martin by Floyd Tolliver placed the latter and his friends and relatives in a dangerous position. They knew the Martins would not pass lightly over the matter. Their numbers and influence made them dangerous adversaries. Floyd Tolliver lived at Farmers, a small village on the Licking River, a station of the Chesapeake & Ohio Railway, which traverses the county and passes through Morehead.

The Tollivers also were a large family. Floyd, believing himself in danger, now turned to his relatives and friends for assistance. They responded promptly, armed and organized. The Martins, the Sizemore's and the Days did likewise, thus dividing the county into four factions, composed of determined, courageous and desperate men.

During the Circuit Court following the murder of Bradley the grand jury returned indictments against John Martin, Floyd Tolliver and Sheriff John C. Day for malicious shooting, wounding and murder. Bail was granted, bonds were readily executed and the cases continued until the next term of court.

In December following the fight of August, 1884, Floyd Tolliver and John Martin, who had recovered from his wounds, came for the first time face to face outside of the court room and were not in custody of the officers, since their fight. They met in a bar room, a place never suitable for enemies to meet. Had both men been duly sober trouble might have been averted. But, flushed with liquor, the old grudge soon got in its work, a dispute arose, their hands reached for their pistols, the shining weapons flashed for a moment, then belched forth fire and flame, a cry, the dull thud of a falling body, Floyd Tolliver lay prostrate upon the floor dead.

Martin was immediately arrested and conveyed to the county jail. To his friends the killing was a shock. They were fully convinced that Craig Tolliver and the other brothers of Floyd Tolliver would seek summary vengeance. Grave fears were entertained for the safety of John Martin in the old jail. Rumors of the organization of a large Tolliver mob increased anxiety and apprehension with each fleeting hour. But, as much as the Tollivers were feared, and the more they threatened, Martin's friends bravely prepared to protect him at all hazards. Thus the aggressiveness of the Tollivers was counteracted by the bold defiance of the Martins.

The County Attorney, Mr. Young, was one of the ablest and most fearless Commonwealth lawyers in Kentucky. By his enemies, and they were numerous, he was regarded as wholly unscrupulous. They refused to credit him with even one pure thought, or action, emanating from a noble impulse. But unbiased investigation of the facts of this matter clearly shows that Mr. Young did his duty in this particular instance. He was perfectly acquainted with the character of the men arrayed against Martin, and was not the man to be deluded by their repeated declarations that the law would be permitted to take its course. At the risk of antagonizing the Tolliver faction against himself Mr. Young promptly directed the removal of John Martin to the Clark County jail at Winchester for safekeeping. County Judge Stewart saw the wisdom of it and issued the order for the removal, which was accomplished without mishap.

As soon as it became known that their intended victim had escaped them, the Tollivers, furious and raging, gathered in large force, spreading terror wherever they appeared. "We can wait, " they said. "There is another day coming. John Martin must be brought back to Morehead for trial and then just wait."

December 10, 1884, was the day set for the examining trial before County Judge Stewart at Morehead. Before that day arrived, the unusual activity of the Tollivers, the ominous collection of all the members and friends of that family, the frequent but secret meetings, had been quietly, but nevertheless keenly observed by Judge Stewart. He was convinced that if Martin were brought back to Rowan County at this time of ferment and excitement he would suffer a violent death at the hands of his enemies, and that any attempt on the part of the officers and friends of the prisoner would precipitate a conflict, the magnitude of which could not be foretold.

In this opinion Attorney Young sustained Judge Stewart. After a careful investigation of the state of affairs the court decided on an indefinite postponement of the trial. The order to the jailer of Clark County, directing him to deliver Martin to officers of Rowan County, was suspended on the 9th day of December, but unfortunately (fateful neglect) the order of suspension was not communicated to the Clark County jailer. The wife of John Martin had been advised of the postponement of the trial. The faithful woman who had already suffered untold anxiety and fear for the safety of her husband, felt relieved and hastened to Winchester to inform him of the action of the Court of Rowan County.

As soon as the Tollivers were informed that the trial would not take place, and that, therefore, Martin would remain at Winchester for an indefinite time; they convened in a council of war to discuss plans of campaign. A raid upon the Winchester jail was suggested, but the leaders, though desperate and brave enough to have attempted and dared anything did not believe that such an undertaking would meet with success. They advised strategy instead of force.

On the 9th of December, on the same day that Judge Stewart canceled the order for delivery of the prisoner by the jailer of Clark County; an order was delivered into the hands of A.M. Bowling, town Marshal at Farmers, directing him to demand Martin from the jailer at Winchester and to convey him to the county jail at Morehead. The order also directed the jailer of Clark County to surrender Martin into the custody of Bowling.

The plot was shrewdly planned. The order, forged, of course, would open the doors of the Winchester jail without difficulty, and the prisoner must, therefore, become an easy victim on his way to Rowan County. Bowling, a Tolliver clansman engaged four other members of it to accompany him to Winchester, Hall, Eastman, Milt and Ed Evans. Four men to convey a handcuffed prisoner! It was deemed best to send a sufficient number to prevent outsiders from interfering in the final act of the inhuman drama staged by Craig Tolliver and his henchmen.

On arriving at the jail at Winchester, Bowling presented his order, which was signed by two Justices of the Peace from Rowan County and which directed the delivery of Martin to Bowling. The order was carefully drawn in the usual form, and had every appearance of genuineness.

A few minutes after John Martin's wife had bidden her husband goodbye at the Winchester jail, Bowling presented his order for the delivery of Martin.

While the wife was at the station awaiting the arrival of the train which was to carry her homeward, little dreaming that she had clasped the hand of her husband warm with life for the last time, the prisoner was aroused by his keeper and told to prepare for his removal to Morehead. Martin at once became suspicious.

He demonstrated against the transfer, but the jailer produced the order. The prisoner pleaded long and earnestly. He explained to the official that he had received definite information through his wife that on account of the danger that awaited him at Morehead the county authorities of Rowan County had indefinitely postponed his removal. He insisted that Bowling and his companions were his deadly enemies; that every surrounding circumstance pointed to treachery, and that his delivery into the hands of Bowling meant nothing neither more nor less than assassination. The jailer turned a deaf ear to his entreaties. He argued that a refusal to comply with the imperative order of the Rowan County Judge would involve him in trouble. He had no right to believe the order forged. It bore the stamp of genuineness.

It seems to us, however, that a more circumspect officer, informed of the conditions and circumstances surrounding the prisoner, acquainted with the dangerous state of affairs in Rowan County as the result of which Martin had been removed to Winchester, would have held the prisoner until he could have communicated with the authorities at Morehead. Disobedience to the court's orders, intended for the protection of a helpless prisoner, could not have been subject to censure, especially when the forgery of the order was later on established. He might easily have verified the genuineness of the paper by telegraph. Blind obedience often works injury. Threatening disasters through blunders of commanding officers have often been averted by the disobedience of inferior officers, who preferred facing Court martial rather than become a party to useless slaughter and defeat.

John Martin was delivered to Bowling and his companions. Securely shackled, he was marched to the train. Doubtless he suffered the same mental agony, as does the man on the way to the scaffold. It was pathetic chance that Mrs. Martin boarded the same train. She entered another coach, entirely ignorant of her husband's presence in the next one.

While this occurred at Winchester, Craig Tolliver and his band had already assembled at Farmers, ready to play their part in the cowardly deed. Armed to the teeth, they were posted at and near the railway station, impatiently awaiting the arrival of the train. The night was dark and disagreeable, perfectly suited for a holdup.

Presently the flash of light pierces the gloom, the shriek of the engine whistle echoes mournfully through the night. You could hear the train that was bearing John Martin thundering toward the station. The airbrakes wheeze, the train slows up; the conductor cries "All out for Farm" He does not finish the call of the station. A pistol is thrust into his face. Armed men board the engine and cover the engineer and fireman. Others enter the coach in whom Martin is sitting, handcuffed, utterly helpless, surrounded by Bowling and his confederates. Martin sees the men enter and instinctively realizes that his end has come. He attempts to rise to his feet. Instantly shots are fired. Martin sinks back upon his seat, lifeless, his "protectors" calmly witnessing the murder.

Martin's wife, in another coach, had up to this time believed her husband secure in his cell at Winchester. But the moment she heard the shots, unaccountable, undeniable dread seized her. Instinctively she rushed to the scene of the tragedy and found her suspicions realized. There lay the blood-covered body of her husband, literally torn to pieces and perforated with leaden messengers of death. All that the faithful, grief stricken wife could do was to order the remains taken on to Morehead. Martin was buried amid a large concourse of sorrowing friends and relatives.

The solemnity of the occasion accorded ill with the many oppressed, yet nonetheless ominous threats of terrible and swift punishment of the murderers. The news of the cowardly assassination spread like wildfire over the county. The war had begun in earnest. From the day John Martin's body was consigned to the grave, the angel of peace departed from Rowan County. For more than three years a reign of terror was to sweep over it with all its attendant horrors, cutting a wide path of desolation and misery.

Deeds of violence now occurred at frequent intervals. All manner of crime went unpunished by the law. The whole machinery of the law was rotten, the officers of the courts being themselves partisans, in some instances very active as such. Mr. Young, the county attorney, was the first to feel the wrath of the Martin faction. While riding along the road on Christi Creek he was shot from ambush and painfully, but not fatally, wounded. The perpetrators of this deed were not definitely known, but Young's friends claimed to have certain information that the men who attempted his assassination had acted under instructions from the Martin faction, which had openly accused Young of playing into the hands of the Tollivers, and had even gone so far as to allege that he had with them connived in the murder of John Martin. Whether he was or was not a Tolliver sympathizer, another murder committed soon afterwards was laid at the door of the Tollivers, to avenge, it was charged, the wounding of Mr. Young.

Under the circumstances this gentleman determined to and did remove from the county where his life was evidently no longer safe. He located in an adjoining county. At the succeeding election his son was elected to the office his father had vacated. The murder above referred to was that of Stewart

Baumgartner. Cook Humphrey, the Republican Sheriff, had appointed him a deputy. On the 17th day of March 1885, Baumgartner rode along Christi Creek, when, almost at the identical spot where Mr. Young had been fired upon, he was shot and instantly killed from ambush. No one was ever indicted for that killing, but it was generally believed, charged and never, denied that Craig Tolliver's subordinates were the murderers.

Shortly after the death of Baumgartner, and during the month of April, 1885, Cook Humphrey and a stranger, afterwards ascertained to have been Ed. Pierce of Greenup County, Ky., appeared on the streets of Morehead, heavily armed and followed by a number of Martin sympathizers. This act of defiance called forth bitter denunciation from the Tollivers and their friends, between who was ex Sheriff Day and Jeff Bowling, men of reckless courage.

The leaders of the opposing factions assembled every available man, and provided them with arms. The most determined preparations were made to fight out their differences on the streets of Morehead. Humphrey's headquarters was at the Carey House; a hotel owned and operated by James Carey, an ex-captain of the Union Army and a very influential citizen.

The Tollivers occupied the Cottage Hotel near the Chesapeake & Ohio Railway depot, then owned by Dr. R.L. Rains. As quickly as possible a message was forwarded to Craig Tolliver absent from Morehead at the time. He came, accompanied by a number of Tollivers from Elliott County. The battle opened fast and furious. A continuous fire from many guns kept the citizens of the town in terror for many hours. The balls whizzed through every portion of the ill-fated village. Storehouses and dwellings were riddled. None dared to enter the streets, or expose his body for an instant.

The Carey House apparently bore the brunt of the firing. Hundreds of balls struck and shattered the slight frame structure. The Tollivers, beside superior numbers, had the advantage of position. Their marksmanship was better, too. Humphrey and his clan soon realized that a charge upon their position would mean their annihilation. So at an opportune moment the Carey House was abandoned and the Tollivers remained in undisputed control.

In spite of the long continued, heavy firing, an unremitting fusillade of many hours' duration, there were no casualties. The battle, however, exercised such a terrifying influence over the peaceable citizens of the town that all could leave. Morehead, in fact the county, was now in a state of anarchy. The matter was reported to the Governor, who immediately ordered General John B. Castleman, then Adjutant General of Kentucky, to Morehead to investigate conditions there and to discover the causes of this shameful lawlessness.

General Castleman, in company with others, went to Morehead and interviewed the adherents of the different factions and leading citizens of the county. This commission, on completing its mission, reported its findings to the Governor. The result was that the leading spirits in the feud were summoned to Louisville, Ky., where a compromise was patched up between the belligerents. Both sides pledged themselves to return home, to lay down their arms and to cease to molest each other. This proceeding brought into prominence H.M. Logan, Judge James Carey and Cook Humphrey as adherents of the Martin faction and Craig Tolliver, Dr. Jerry Wilson and others as the Tolliver faction leaders.

The agreement entered into at Louisville, intended to restore peace, and affected the opposite result. It prevented prosecution of either side for the Morehead riot. The leniency extended by the authorities merely emboldened and encouraged the warring parties the truce was violated by both sides within a short time after it had been agreed to. The factions charged each other with insincerity, of secretly maintaining armed bands and preparing for renewed hostilities. Within a few weeks after the compromise at Louisville, conditions in Rowan were as bad as ever, nay worse.

As we have stated, the shooting of Young, the County Attorney, had been charged to the Martin faction. In retaliation for this crime the Tollivers had murdered Sheriff Humphrey's deputy, Baumgartner. Subsequent developments then seemed to directly implicate Cook Humphrey in the shooting of Young, and this led to a renewal of active hostilities. It appears that immediately after the treaty at Louisville, Ed Pierce, the man who had so mysteriously appeared on the streets of Morehead in company with Cook Humphrey on the day of the riot, was arrested in Greenup County and taken to Bath County for trial on a charge of robbery. A jury found him guilty. He was sentenced to the penitentiary for a long term. While confined in jail previous to his trial, he admitted his participation in the shooting of Mr. Young, implicating also Ben Rayborn of Carter County, a man but little known in Rowan County.

In his confession Pierce claimed to have been employed to kill Mr. Young by the sisters and family of John Martin, and that Sheriff Humphrey and Baumgartner, his deputy, had aided and assisted in arranging the details of the plot. Humphrey and the Martins indignantly denied every word of Pierces confession, and asserted that he had been bribed by Mr. Young to make it for the purpose of destroying the prestige of the Martin family in the county, and to furnish the excuse for further outrages.

The Tollivers now put Humphrey and the Martin family under constant surveillance. The Martin homestead, situated about one mile from Morehead, became an object of special vigilance. Finally, on the evening of the 27th day of July 1885, the Tolliver spies reported to their leader at Morehead that two men had been seen around the Martin home. Instantly everything was in commotion at the Tolliver headquarters. Craig Tolliver, Jeff Bowling, T.A.

Day and others, all sworn enemies of the Martins, surrounded the homestead in the dark of night and remained on watch until morning.

Shortly after daylight a stranger, afterwards recognized as Ben Rayborn, in company of Sue Martin, a young woman of much native sense and energy emerged from the house and "robbed" a beehive in the yard without having discovered the enemy. Rayborn was heavily armed. His presence convinced the Tollivers that Cook Humphrey was in the house; they now determined upon open attack. But to avoid possible failure of the plot it was deemed necessary to increase the force. A messenger was hurriedly dispatched to Morehead.

A short time afterwards the Tollivers had assembled a force of twenty-five or thirty men, among who were many of the most violent men of Rowan County. At nine o'clock Craig Tolliver had stationed this force at every point of vantage. Then he and Bowling appeared at the front door with Winchester rifles gleaming in the sunlight. For the first time the inmates of the house seemed aware of the presence of the enemy. There was apparently no chance of escape. Every door was securely guarded.

The brave Martin girls who demanded an explanation for the intrusion met Tolliver at the door. Tolliver demanded the surrender of Cook Humphrey and any other man or men that might be with him. The girls stoutly denied the presence of any one save the members of the family. Tolliver knew this to be false. With his own eyes he had seen Rayborn that morning. He charged the girls with duplicity and forced his way into the house. No one was found on the first floor. Then they attempted search of the upper story. At the stairway a shotgun suddenly belched forth fire and flame into the faces of the Tollivers.

Craig's face and part of his body was filled with shot, the gunstock shivered to pieces in his hand. He sank upon the steps and rolled helplessly at the feet of his companions. Bowling miraculously escaped unhurt. Craig Tolliver was immediately placed upon a horse and sent to Morehead for repairs. The others, not daring to force the stairway, went outside and contented themselves with firing through the doors and windows. The fusillade continued incessantly for a long time. Black smoke hung like a cloud over the premises.

If the Tollivers hoped to force the surrender of Humphrey and his companion by mere intimidation, they soon saw their mistake. These two men were brave to the core. Besides, they preferred to die fighting rather to being mercilessly butchered as helpless prisoners. They remembered the fate of John Martin. Finally Humphrey managed to make him heard through the din and crash of battle. He informed his assailants that he was there in the house and that by virtue of his office as sheriff of the county none but the coroner had the legal right to arrest him.

The Tollivers sneered at this speech. They had not come to uphold the law; they had succeeded in trapping the enemy, and meant to use the advantage they had gained. Hours thus passed. All day the guns roared into and from the house. The sun was sinking rapidly toward the western horizon; the shades of evening grew longer. As long as daylight lasted the assailants had kept covered and protected, held at bay by the brave defenders. But in the dark of night, the end must come. They could not prevent a simultaneous attack from the entire force of the assailants. Surrounded on every side, escape seemed well near impossible. Yet Humphrey essayed to make a sortie with his companion, hoping thereby to draw the fire of the enemy upon themselves and to thus at least relieve the women in the house of further danger of death, which had threatened them every moment throughout that long day.

It was a desperate undertaking, with ninety-nine chances in a hundred against its success. But Humphrey was brave, and so was Rayborn. As expected, the instant they emerged from the house a shower of balls greeted them. They ran for their lives. Rayborn sank, rose and fell again, to rise no more. His body was riddled. Humphrey, however, seemed possessed of a charmed life. Though his clothing was torn to shreds, his body received not a scratch. Satisfied now that there were no more men in the house, the Tolliver clan crowned their infamous day's work by setting fire to it.

The inmates escaped without even necessary clothing. The body of Rayborn was left lying where it had fallen until the next day, protected from mutilation by dogs and hogs by a rail pen, which had been built around it by the heroic Martin girls. The excitement that prevailed in the county when the news of the cowardly attack upon the Martin home became known can better be imagined than described. The lover of law and order was terror stricken. The question was asked in whispers "Where will it all end."

The County Judge was a well meaning man, but utterly incompetent as an officer, possessing none of the qualifications for such an office in a county like Rowan at such a time of lawlessness and anarchy. He was weak and timid. Always in fear for his life, he completely lost his head. Warrants were at last issued upon the affidavits of the Martin girls against Craig Tolliver, Jeff Bowling and a number of others, charging them with murder and arson. An examining trial followed. At that time such trials were held before two justices of the peace. One was said to be a Martin sympathizer; the other stood accused of being under the thumb of the Tollivers.

The court's decision gave color to these suspicions. One of the magistrates decided for commitment of the prisoners to jail without bail; the other declared that no offense had been proven. Under the law then existing this disagreement of the court permitted the murderers to go free. The trial was a pronounced farce. Afterwards some of the parties were indicted by the grand jury for arson, but none was convicted and the murder charges against them all fell. Jeff Bowling, one of the most desperate of the Tolliver faction, removed from the county of Rowan a short time afterward, and settled in Ohio, where he continued his career of crime, evidently believing that there, as well as in Kentucky, none dared molest him.

He saw his mistake too late. It appears that his mother-in-law had married a wealthy farmer named Douglas, of Licking County, Ohio. It had been due to the persuasion of Douglas that Bowling left Kentucky and settled in or near his Ohio kinsman. Bowling had resided there but a short time when Douglas was found one morning in his barn murdered. The finger of suspicion pointed to Bowling as the only one who had a tangible motive for the commission of the crime. He was promptly indicted, tried and sentenced to death, but the sentence was finally commuted to life imprisonment. He served seven years of his time and moved to Texas.

Humphrey, after his miraculous escape from the Martin house, had become thoroughly convinced that it was impossible for him to longer continue in the office of sheriff and resigned, William Ramey being appointed and qualified in his stead. Craig Tolliver for a time absented himself from Rowan County. He turned up in jail at Cincinnati, imprisoned on the charge of robbery. He was tried, acquitted and returned to Rowan County, when trouble started anew. Several killings occurred in the county during the year, some of which had, however, only remote connection with the feud.

John G. Hughes was killed by a mob styling themselves "regulators." One Mack Bentley killed Wiley Tolliver, son of L.H.B. Tolliver, about Christmas, 1885, during a drunken row. Early in 1886, the murder of Whit Pelfrey, at Elliottsville, Rowan County, came near precipitating another outbreak. He was stabbed and killed by Tom Goodan, brother of S.B. Goodan, a prominent Tolliver man and brother-in-law of Jay, Bud and Wiley Tolliver. Pelfrey, known as a strong Martin sympathizer, was an influential citizen and wealthy. Goodan was tried for this murder, but acquitted.

The year 1886 brought with it an annual election at which all county officers were to be chosen. Each faction had its candidates in the field. It may, therefore, be easily imagined that neutral citizens remained in a state of constant anxiety and apprehension.

Cook Humphrey and Craig Tolliver roamed through the county at the head of large forces, frequently entering the town of Morehead and parading the streets in defiance of each other. On July 2nd, 1886, it being County Court day, a warrant of arrest was placed in the hands of Sheriff Ramey for the arrest of Humphrey, who was in town that day. The officer went in search of and found him near the store of H.M. Logan.

An altercation ensued between the men; both drew their pistols and began firing. Friends of both parties became involved and the shooting became general. When the fight was over it was found that the sheriff and his son and deputy, were both dangerously wounded, while W.O. Logan, H.M. Logan's son, a youth hardly twenty years of age, was killed. Immediately after the fight the factions retired to their headquarters and pre- pared for another conflict.

The County Judge was prevailed upon to demand troops. His request was readily granted and a detachment of State Guards, commanded by Major K. W. McKee of Lawrenceburg, hastened to the scene of the trouble.

When July 3rd came, the citizens, women and children, trembled with fear of a bloody conflict. At the quarters of the factions guns and pistols were cleaned, oiled and loaded, cartridge belts filled every preparation made for battle. Then the long drawn notes of a bugle floated in the morning air, the astonished people peered through the windows and beheld in the courthouse yard a long line of soldiers, their guns and bayonets glistening in the morning sun. There was a sigh of relief danger had passed for the moment. The troops remained at Morehead until some time in August. It was due to their presence that the election passed off without violence and bloodshed.

When Circuit Court convened, the Honorable Ahser C. Caruth, Commonwealth Attorney of the Jefferson Circuit Court, and afterwards member of Congress, represented the Commonwealth from the Louisville District. As at this time practically every citizen in the county was aligned on one side or the other, it seemed impossible to secure juries that would try cases impartially and without prejudice. This state of affairs did not escape the attention of Mr. Caruth. The result of his investigations of affairs in Rowan County resulted in a nolle prosequis, qualified by certain conditions, of the charges against the Tollivers and Humphrey. His proceeding in this respect is contained in the following report to Judge Cole, presiding judge of the Circuit Court: Hon. A.E. Cole, Judge of the Rowan Circuit Court.

Under your appointment I have acted as Commonwealth Attorney pro tempore at the special July and present August term of the Rowan Circuit Court. I have given the felony docket, over which alone, under the present law, I have jurisdiction, careful study and attention. I have also investigated as thoroughly as a stranger to the people of Rowan County could do in the limited time of my service, the causes which led to the present unhappy condition of affairs, and have sought to find a remedy for the evils afflicting this people. I find it to be the opinion of the law abiding citizens of all parties that the public peace could be best secured by the continued absence from the county of Rowan of the acknowledged and recognized leaders of the two rival factions - Craig Tolliver and Cook Humphrey.

Against the former there is now pending one felony charge, that of false arrest and imprisonment. Against Humphrey there are three indictments for felony on the docket, each for conspiring, etc., to commit personal violence. I have the written request of each of these persons accused to suspend further proceedings in their cases, coupled with a promise on the part of each to leave the county of Rowan never to return unless, temporarily, to attend the funeral of some immediate relative.

The persons charged to have been injured by their acts also request this disposition of the pending cases. It is the opinion of the members of the grand jury now in session, and of the vast majority of the citizens of the county, that this disposition of the cases will do much to restore peace and confidence to the community. After full consultation with the members of the bar residing here or practicing here, with the commander of the forces now stationed at the county seat, and with citizens of high position and authority in the Commonwealth, and considering the uncertainty of the criminal trials, I am convinced that this is the best available method to secure the end in view. No harm can, by this means, be done the State, because, should the agreement be violated, the cases can at once be set for trial and prosecutions made.

The following written agreements were then signed and attested: Asher G. Caruth, Commonwealth's Attorney pro tempore, 14th Judicial District: I request you to suspend any further proceedings in the cases now pending in the Rowan Circuit Court against me, and promise that I will remain away from the county of Rowan permanently. Should I ever return to said county I am willing that the cases shall be re-docketed and the trials proceed. I will leave said, county on or before the 8th day of August, A. D. 1886. In this agreement I reserve the right, in the event of the death of any of my immediate relatives, to return to attend their burial, but I must immediately thereafter leave the county to permanently remain away.

(Signed) Craig Tolliver

Attest: D.E. Logan

A similar agreement was prepared and signed by W.C. Humphrey, attested by G.A. Cassidy.

We do not wish to criticize Mr. Caruth's course in this matter, but it occurs to us, and must occur to the reader, that the practice of compromising with outlaws proves a weak kneed administration of the law. It seems that a man or set of men may terrorize a community as it pleases them, and then demand of the authorities' immunity for crimes, on certain conditions prescribed by the criminals. Mr. Caruth acted for the best interests of the community, as he believed.

Aware those juries were partial or prejudiced; he realized that trials in Rowan County of either of the factions would result in injustice one way or another.

The Grand Juries were corrupt and accustomed to wreak vengeance on some and white washing others. The selection of trial juries was so palpably unfair that visiting lawyers commented upon it and afterward testified before the legislative committee to that fact. Several court officers were undisguised partisans.

It seems to us, however, that these cases might have been removed from the county and tried elsewhere upon a change of venue. At any rate, the compromise affected by Mr. Caruth proved not only unsatisfactory, but also ill advised. The success of his scheme was founded upon the belief that the parties to the agreement would adhere to the pledge to leave the county. He did not understand the character of Craig Tolliver. To secure his signature to an agreement that would put an enemy out of his way was one thing, to make him keep it, another.

Tolliver remained absent from Morehead long enough to assure himself that the indictments against him were dismissed, when he promptly returned. Although the compromise was based upon the understanding that if either returned except under the conditions recited in the agreement that the indictments against the party so returning should be re-docketed and revived, this was never done. Tolliver was free to continue his career of crime. Humphrey kept his word, and never violated his pledge. He sold out his earthly possessions in Rowan County and bade farewell to his native State. Previous to his election as sheriff Humphrey had been a highly esteemed citizen, a man of exemplary character, of amiable disposition. His fatal connection with the feud was mainly due to his unfortunate selection of Stewart Baumgartner as his deputy.

The latter was a citizen of Elliott County, where he had a reputation for violence and desperation. Pursuing the same course in Rowan, Humphrey's association with him made him many enemies. Baumgartner's connection with the Martin faction compromised Humphrey; thus step-by-step he was thrown into the whirlpool of trouble. The formerly quiet, inoffensive citizen grew dangerous and violent; the dormant, unholy passion of revenge was aroused. Humphrey became for the time being a character dreaded by those that opposed him. At the time of his participation in the feud he was yet in his twenties and unmarried. After leaving Kentucky he went west, never to return to his native heath until after the death of Craig Tolliver and his followers, and then only on special business.

With Humphrey gone, the Martin faction practically disbanded. Had Tolliver observed the treaty stipulations as faithfully and honestly as did Humphrey, this chapter might end here? The writer would be spared the unpleasant task of continuing the record of violence, murder and anarchy. It is evident that Tolliver had entered into this agreement with the avowed purpose of violating it. He had every reason to believe that Humphrey would observe it. With him out of the way, there stood no one to dispute Tolliver's undisputed sway in the county, especially at Morehead.

His adherents remained faithful and joined him. They did as they pleased, in fact had things their own way. If the authorities did not dare molest them, who should? A few of the citizens, who had attempted a mild protest against Craig Tolliver's dictatorship, were easily intimidated by keeping them in constant fear of death or destruction of their property. Saloons were opened and operated without license. Magistrates refused to issue warrants, knowing that such an act would forfeit their lives. Had the warrants been issued, no officers could have been persuaded to execute them. The residences and grog shops of the Tollivers resembled and were arsenals.

An effective and favorite method of Craig Tolliver to rid himself of any, to him, undesirable citizens, was to send a written communication to them, setting forth the fact that Rowan County could dispense with their presence, and that on a certain day in the near future certain funerals would take place unless they were gone from the county. A funeral is not a pleasant function at any time, and the prospect of one's own set for a definite time, has a tendency with many persons to try hard to avoid it, if possible.

It was, therefore, not surprising that party's thus notified preferred absence from the county to being principals at funerals. A few regarded those letters as idle and meaningless threats, but the sincerity of the advice could no longer be doubted or questioned when several prophesied funerals did take place. To detail the circumstances of the various killings that occupied during that stormy period of Rowan County would prove tedious.

Suffice it to say, that from the first Monday in August 1884, to the 22nd of July 1887, twenty-three men were killed in Rowan County. No convictions were secured for any of these murders. But of this later on October 20th, 1886, H.M. Logan was shot from ambush in the streets of Morehead, while walking from his place of business to his residence. The wound was, dangerous but not fatal. Judge Carey came in for a full share of the enemy's hatred and vengeance. Parties armed with needle guns and large caliber Winchesters frequently fired into his hotel at night. His house assumed the appearance of having been struck by a cyclone. Windows and doors had been completely shot away and the walls perforated in a thousand places. It required neither doors nor windows to admit daylight.

The Exchange Hotel shared a similar fate. H.C. Powers, another Humphrey adherent, managed it. This kind of argument was convincing, more forcible than words or letters. Powers and Carey both felt a sudden desire to remove from the atmosphere of Morehead, concluding that Covington, Kentucky, possessed greater allurements for the time being than did their home town. Both remained away from the county until after the bloody, final battle at

Morehead in 1887. Unfortunately, we have no authentic account of the leave taking between the Tollivers, Carey and Powers. It must have been very affectionate, since the Tollivers had exhibited such concern for their safety, comfort and health as to persuade them so urgently to remove to a happier and better land.

Howard Logan (H.M.), too, had enough of this joke about funeral predictions. He could not see the point of it, and concluded that Ashland, on the banks of the beautiful Ohio River, would be the proper place to recover from his labors and see the world. He also remained away until after the annihilation of the Tollivers. There were a number of others who seemed suddenly seized with a fever to emigrate. Among them were John R. Powers, James E. Clark, a prominent lawyer, who found a more congenial home at Unionville, Clark County, Missouri; James Brain, a brother-in-law of Judge Carey. R.C. Humphrey, brother of Cook Humphrey; both of whom settled in Missouri. Many others "scouted" in neighboring counties until the return of peace.

Judge Tussey, brother-in-law of the murdered John Martin, on the advice and persuasion of his wife, remained absent in Carter County and returned only to take part in the final drama. Nearly all of the parties, who were thus driven from the county, were men of wealth and business capacity. Removals continued.

The magnitude of the exodus may be realized by examining the figures giving the population of the county seat, Morehead, from 1885 until the early part of 1887. In 1885 Morehead was a flourishing town of more than seven hundred inhabitants. Within two years this figure was reduced to less than three hundred. More than half the population had removed. Private residences and storehouses stood empty, with windows nailed up or were taken possession of by the Tollivers whenever it suited their fancy. The Tollivers made up the population. Tollivers filled the offices of police judge and town marshal.

On June 1st, 1887, Craig Tolliver had the entire town under absolute control. He was elected police and judge without opposition. He did a driving business, selling whiskey, without license, of course. The law as to obtaining license to sell liquor applied not to him. He was above the law. He took possession of the Exchange Hotel, which H.C. Powers had left without a tenant, by right of conquest. Why should he have troubled himself with renting property when houses stood empty, and he was monarch of the town! The property of his enemies was the spoils of war.

Its owners placed the Central Hotel at the disposal of Tolliver; the former leased it to Bunk Mannin and his brother, Jim Mannin. These two were Craig Tolliver's constant associates. He had brought them from Elliott County. Knowing their reputation as desperadoes, he created them his bodyguard. Bunk Mannin, blood thirsty, brutal, but courageous, believed he could serve his chieftain best by capturing the office of town marshal. He set himself up as candidate and was elected without a whisper of opposition. As town marshal and hotelkeeper, he opened a saloon at the Central Hotel, operating it in the manner of the one run by Craig Tolliver, in violation of the law. Bud Tolliver was made a member of the town council. Craig Tolliver's triumph was now complete.

The midnight carousels, the continuous discharges of Winchester rifles and pistols, made night hideous. Persons of unquestionable courage grew nervous. At this period the exodus of the inhabitants was greatest. Social functions were out of the question.

Adjutant General Hill says in his report to the Governor, after the final battle of July, 1887: "One night while I was there the young people of Morehead had a social at the home of a prominent citizen, and I was told that it was the first event of the kind which had occurred in the little town for years." The Tollivers controlled the court and the grand juries. A witness daring enough to indict them for their many offenses was certain to be indicted for some imaginary offense in return for his audacity.

Thus during one court, shortly after the "shooting up" of the Carey House, two daughters of Howard Logan testified before the grand jury and indicted one Dr. Wilson for participating in the riot. The same evening the grand jury returned indictments against the two young ladies for "false swearing." The secrets of the grand jury leaked constantly. Every word of testimony uttered before it was promptly and minutely reported to the Tollivers. Mrs. Martin, who had been a witness against them on several charges, was indicted for sending a poisoned turkey to a Tolliver sympathizer. Is it a wonder that Attorney General Hardin stigmatized the whole machinery of justice in the county as "rotten"?

Is it a wonder that crime was rampant and of daily occurrence? Is it a wonder that out- raged manhood at last took the law in its own hand and annihilated the outlaws? Sometime in the latter part of 1886, or early part of 1887, H.M. Keeton, constable of Morehead precinct, was shot and killed by Bud Tolliver. Keeton, too, had been duly served with notice of the date of his funeral. Remaining in the county, he furnished the body.

W.N. Wicher was shot and killed by John Trumbo, a Tolliver man. At the February term of the Rowan Circuit Court (IW7) Dr. Henry S. Logan, R.M. McClure, John B. and W.H. Logan and Lewis Rayborn, were indicted for conspiracy to murder Circuit Court Judge A.E. Cole, James H. Sallee, Commonwealth's Attorney, and Z.T. Young. All the parties indicted were prominent citizens and of such a character that those not prejudiced against, and acquainted with them, at once declared the charges false. The entire transaction bore the earmarks of a shrewdly laid plot to rid the county of these men, who had become objectionable to Czar Craig Tolliver because they had dared to criticize his rule. The indicted parties were arrested and confined in jail, their bail having been placed at an exorbitant sum. They were hustled off to Lexington for "safekeeping."

John B. and W.H. Logan gave bond and returned to there home, about four miles distant from Morehead. Their father remained in prison. When it became known that James Pelfrey was the chief witness against them, it seemed easy to see through the whole affair. Pelfreys black character was well known by some of the Tolliver clan, and to this unscrupulous man they had turned to affect their villainous conspiracy. A suitable story was concocted and rehearsed. With it Pelfrey appeared before the grand jury, and loaded upon his sin stained soul the dastardly, black crime of perjury. After their return home the Logan boys lived quietly and alone, taking charge of the farm in their father's absence.

W.H. Logan (Billy) was a consumptive, twenty-five years old, and almost reduced to a skeleton by the dread disease. His brother, J.B. Logan (Jack) was a youth of eighteen. On the 7th of June, 1887, a disreputable character named Hiram Cooper, who lived in the neighborhood of the Logan boys, came to Morehead and swore out a warrant against the Logan boys and their cousin, A.W. Logan, charging them with confederating and banding together for the purpose of murdering him (Cooper). This act was in pursuance of the original plot to rid the county of the family, which, however, had failed to some extent when the boys had succeeded in giving bail and were released from prison. Craig Tolliver, the police judge, issued the warrants. They were placed in the hands of his confederate, Town Marshal Bunk Mannin, who summoned a posse of ten men to assist him in the execution of the warrants against the two boys. Among these brave officers were Deputy Sheriff George Hogg, Bud Tolliver, Jay Tolliver, Cal Tolliver, Hiram Cooper and one Young.

Completely ignorant of the impending danger, the boys were found at home. The first warning they had of the approach of the assassins, under the guise of officers, was the rapid firing of guns. The boys, terrified, ran upstairs, Mannin and Craig Tolliver rushing after them. Jack Logan seized a shotgun, and over the earnest protest of his brother, Billy, fired into the body of Mannin, inflicting a painful, but, unfortunately, not fatal wound. Mannin and Craig Tolliver retreated from the house, while the boys waited tremblingly, with bated breath, for developments. They saw there was no hope for them. The smell of burning wood and clouds of smoke told them of their peril. By order of Judge Tolliver the posse committals had built a fire on the porch intending to burn the house, and thus force the boys to come out. The crackling of flames, the shouts and cruel, derisive laughter of the brutal band outside presented a scene such as we read of with horror in the stories of the Indian wars.

Deputy Sheriff Hogg then requested permission to extinguish the flames. The other "representatives of the law" consenting, a parley was held. Hogg went into the house and offered the boys the alternative of surrender or death by fire. They naturally chose the former, hoping against hope that some miracle might yet ' save them, or that, perhaps, their appearing unarmed, might move the band with compassion and mercy. However, before leaving the house, they wished assurance that their lives should be protected. Deputy Sheriff Hogg reported to Craig Tolliver, and that redoubtable officer of the Commonwealth authorized him to promise them protection. This assurance was then communicated to the boys, supplemented by the personal guaranty of Sheriff Hogg. The boys determined to leave the house. Billy Logan went downstairs in company of Hogg. The younger boy was yet reluctant to trust himself into the hands of Craig Tolliver and Bunk Mannin, the town marshal, but being again assured that no harm should come to him, he, too, followed and emerged into the yard.

They were led away some fifty feet from the house to near a spring. Their John Mannin opened fire upon the elder boy, shooting him in the back. This was the signal for a general fusillade by Craig Tolliver, Bunk Mannin and others. The boys fell dead. Not satisfied with their deaths, the heartless assassins, among whom Town Marshal Mannin was the most ferocious, trampled the prostrate forms, stamped them, and poured volley after volley into the dead bodies, thus mutilating them beyond recognition. They were left lying where they had fallen, a gory, shapeless mass, the glassy eyes upturned to the sky, in mute appeal to God to avenge this horrible assassination. God saw and retribution followed close upon the heels of the inhuman wretches.

Deputy Sheriff Hogg testified afterwards that he ran away as soon as the firing began. The murderers joined him, however, before he had reached town. On the brow of a hill overlooking Morehead Craig Tolliver halted the red handed band and instructed them all to tell the same tale that the boys were killed in resisting arrest, and that their killing had been an absolute necessity.

On the following day D. Boone Logan, a cousin of the murdered boys, accompanied by H.M. (Hiram) Pigman and A.P. Perry, went to the Logan homestead, and found and cared for the mangled remains of his relatives. On that evening, upon their return home, they were warned that they would share a similar fate in the event they attended the funeral. Up to the time of the murder of the Logan boys neither D. Boone Logan nor Pigman had taken any active part in the feudal strife, indeed they had carefully kept aloof from any act or speech that might in any way connect them either directly or indirectly with the faction.

Boone Logan had attested the agreement signed by Craig Tolliver to remove from the county. But beyond this he had remained neutral. Not content, however, with foully murdering his young relatives, Craig Tolliver sent to Boone Logan the exasperating message that he must leave, that he, Tolliver, would rent his house, and hire Logan's wife out to make a living for her children. By threatening D.B. Logan, Craig Tolliver made the mistake of his life. He conjured up a storm, which passed, soon beyond his power to control. When it broke loose in all its fury on the 22nd day of June, and the streets of Morehead ran red with blood, the desperadoes experienced at last the lash of an avenging God.

Boone Logan made futile efforts to have the murderers arrested. After several days had elapsed, Bunk Mannin, the town marshal, went to Logan and told him that he wished to have a trial, and that the Tollivers were also ready for trial. "But, said Mannin, "it must be understood that we attend court with our Winchesters." The Tollivers also notified Judge Stewart that they wished a trial, to which request Judge Stewart made answer that he "would not hold a bogus trial" and refused to try the case. Logan, Pigman and A.P. Perry, in danger of their lives, yet burning with indignation, entered into a solemn compact to affect the arrest and trial of all the parties engaged in the murder of the Logan boys. A resolution made by such men as Boone Logan and his friends meant something more than mere words.

They, too, were men of action. They went to work in the preparation of their plan with coolness and circumspection. Caution was needed indeed. They first attached to their cause a number of men upon whom they could rely. Meetings were held at secret places. Boone Logan was at once chosen as the leader in the enterprise. In the prime of manhood, of fine physique and intelligent, he was just the man to place at the head of such a hazardous undertaking. Combining indomitable courage with prudence, sagacity and coolness, he was also a man of unflinching determination. Such was the man with whom the Tollivers now had to deal.

Educated, a lawyer of prominence, polished, and a quiet gentleman, one would scarcely have picked him out as the man to oppose the outlaws, to attack them in their very stronghold and give them battle. Logan and Pigman avoided being seen in each other's company, yet the Tollivers by some means had learned of their secret meetings, and, growing suspicious, began hunting them high and low. To relate the many narrow escapes these two men had from death would fill pages. The Tollivers patrolled every road, passing trains were searched, and inquiries made everywhere, and insulting messages sent to Logan's family. Shrewdly he avoided any encounter, but with dogged determination continued his preparations.

On the 16th day of June, Boone Logan eluded the vigilance of the Tollivers and succeeded in reaching Frankfort, Ky., where he asked for, and was accorded, an interview with Governor Knott. To him Logan related the existing conditions in Rowan County, the despotism exercised by Craig, Tolliver and his associates in crime; the horrible murder of the Logan boys, for that no one had as yet been molested, and asked for troops to affect the capture of the outlaws. The Governor listened attentively to Mr. Logan's representations, but replied that he had already sent soldiers to Morehead at the cost of many thousands of dollars to the State, with no other result than aiding courts in committing travesties of justice; that under the circumstances he could not see his way clear to repeat his experiences with that county.

He then asked Logan what percent of the population was actually engaged in the trouble, and on receiving reply, answered that the good citizens being so largely in the majority, they should be able to themselves put down lawlessness. Logan admitted that he could find a number of citizens who would be willing to aid him in arresting the outlaws if they could secure the necessary arms. He asked the Governor for the loan of a few guns from the arsenal at Frankfort, offering to give satisfactory security for their safe return. The Governor explained that such a course was unwarranted and a matter beyond his control. Logan's face turned almost livid for a moment. He did not blame the Governor, who acted under the law. But he became exasperated at the thought that a band of murderers were under the law permitted to remain in undisputed possession of his county, his home, while the Governor seemed without authority to come to the rescue of order and to maintain the dignity of the law.

Courts had refused to do their duty; officers championed openly the cause of the murderers; peaceable citizens had been driven from their homes anarchy reined supreme. These thoughts filled his brain. Before his mind's eye appeared the mangled remains of his cousins. He feared for his wife and children at Morehead. His home might at this moment be reduced to ashes and its inmates burned or hot. The young man's eyes gleamed with a dangerous fire. His lips quivered while the strong heart beat almost audibly with excitement, indignation and utter disgust. At last he spoke, slowly, firmly, every word full of meaning.

It was then he made his famous reply, so often repeated and commented upon: "Governor," he said, "I have but one home and but one hearth. From this these outlaws and their friends have driven me. They have foully murdered my kinsmen. I have not before engaged in any of their difficulties but now I propose to take a hand and retake my fireside or die in the effort." Future events proved that these words were uttered for a purpose other than mere dramatic effect. The flashing eye told plainly of the passions that had been kindled in his heart, and the Governor could not but admire the man's just indignation and determination to do what the highest authorities in the State could not do.

The action of Governor Knott in refusing to send troops to Rowan County has been criticized by those ignorant of the law and the powers of the Governor in such cases. The law lays down the scope of his authority. The power of the county had not been exhausted in bringing about, or attempting, the apprehension of the criminals. He had already responded with troops to protect the court only to find that the authorities showed the white feather; that compromises with criminals had been entered into; that juries and officers were corrupt, and when trials had occurred had proved a farce. No doubt in his heart he wished for Logan's success. The man had made futile attempts to live peaceably. Now he intended to act in self-defense. The government cannot help him. He must therefore help himself.

A man's home, no matter how humble it may be, is sacred as the King's palace in the eyes of the ancient common law. To defend it from intrusions and attack is man's God given right, his duty; Boone Logan set about to retake his fireside. After leaving Frankfort, Logan hastened to Cincinnati, Ohio, where he purchased several hundred dollars' worth of Winchester rifles, pistols, shotguns, and an ample supply of ammunition. These were boxed and shipped as sawmill fixtures and consigned to a small station (Gate's) in Rowan County, some miles from Morehead. Immediately upon his return to Rowan County Logan summoned his friends. They responded with a will. Many came from the neighboring counties, except Elliott County, which section sympathized strongly with the Tollivers, whose relatives were strong there.

Sheriff Hogg was placed in possession of the warrants against Craig Tolliver and his confederates, charging them with the recent murders of the Logan boys (June 7th). It was definitely and explicitly agreed upon and arranged that the sheriff should demand the surrender of the Tollivers, and only in case of their refusal to comply were the citizens to take a hand. This, course, was a mere matter of form. It was easy to predict to a certainty that the Tollivers would not obey the demand of surrender by the officers. That had been tried too often before.

Yet the Logan faction desired to exhaust all lawful means before resorting to bloodshed. Sheriff Hogg was instructed to demand the surrender and upon its refusal to retreat in order to insure his personal safety, and to give the forces under Boone Logan an opportunity to enforce the demand. Thus far all went well.

When the morning of June 22nd came, bright and beautiful, everything was in readiness for the coming struggle. Logan, with some of his men, was stationed near the Chesapeake & Ohio Railway Depot. Just across, at the business place of Vinton & Pigman, Hiram Pigman, with six or seven men, stood in readiness to act in concert with Logan. On the opposite side of the town another detachment was carefully posted in concealment. The Tollivers were completely surrounded. Strange to say, with all their vigilance, they had remained in utter ignorance of Logan's final preparations. They despised Logan. His frequent absences from home had been attributed to fear.

Of his visit to Frankfort and his purchase of arms at Cincinnati they knew nothing. It was late in the morning of the 22nd, when an accident revealed to them their danger, though the knowledge came too late to enable their escape. The wife of a railroad man was a visiting friend at Morehead. Her husband had noticed bodies of armed men closing in upon the town. He also knew of the large shipment of arms to Gate's station. Anxious for the safety of his wife, after his suspicions had been aroused, he telegraphed her to leave Morehead at once, that a battle was impending without doubt. This information was conveyed to the Tollivers, who immediately prepared for the attack. Thus it happened that when the battle commenced, Logan and his men were put upon the defensive instead of the offensive, as they had anticipated.

The Logan forces awaited the appearance of the sheriff to demand the surrender of the Tollivers. He failed to arrive. The sheriff afterward testified that armed men from entering the town had prevented him. Be that as it may, the fight opened without him, and during the battle neither he nor his son participated. Logan, unaware that his plans had been betrayed to the Tollivers, attempted to communicate with his friend Pigman at the latter's store. He dispatched a young man, William Bryant, with a note. To his surprise, the Tollivers suddenly appeared, armed to the teeth, and opened fire upon Bryant. The boy fled for life and escaped without a wound. Logan and Pigman, finding their plans discovered, and the sheriff having failed put in his appearance, now commenced the work they had cut out for themselves and their friends to perform.

Firing began from every direction every man shot independently, as best he could. Each part of the town became a separate battlefield. The noncombatants sought safety in flight or in the shelter of their homes. Black clouds of smoke hung over the ill-fated town; the air was stifling with the smell of sulpher. The grim monster of civil war raged in all its fury. Well might we say with Chalmers: 'O, the miseries of war! We recoil with horror at the destruction of a single individual by some deed of violence. When we see a man in the prime of health suddenly struck down by some deadly aim, the sight of the lifeless body haunts us for days and weeks, and the shock experienced, only time can wear away.

"The scene stands before us in daytime, is the subject of our dreams, and spreads a gloom which time can only disperse." It is painful to dwell on the distressing picture of one individual, but multiply it, and think of the agonies of dying men, as goaded by pain, they grasp the cold ground with convulsive energy, or another, faint with the loss of blood, his pulse ebbs low, and the gathering paleness spreads itself over his countenance; or, wrapping himself round in despair, he can only mark by a few feeble quivering, that life still lurks and lingers in his lacerated body; or, lifting up a faded eye, he casts a look of imploring helplessness for that succor which no sympathy can yield."

The moment the battle opened, Logan became the target for many guns from the concealed Tollivers. The balls fell all around him; plowed up the ground at his feet and hissed by his ears. Craig Tolliver and his confederates instinctively singled him out as their most dangerous adversary and made every effort to kill him. The details of the battle are authentically recorded in the report of Ernest McPherson, captain of a detachment of the Louisville Legion, to the Adjutant General of Kentucky, Sam E. Hill, which report was transmitted to the Governor and reported to the Legislature. (See documents 1887, No. 23).

As the Tollivers were coming back, Boone Logan commenced firing. He was at once deserted by the men with him, but continued the fire, which was returned by the two Tollivers, Craig and Jay, until their Winchester rifles and pistols were empty. They ran from below the depot to the American House, Craig Tolliver's hotel, and obtaining a fresh supply of ammunition, were joined by Bud, Andy, Cal and Cate Tolliver, Cooper and others. All then started on the run for the Central Hotel. Andy was the first to reach that building by going through alleys and back ways. Bud Tolliver, Cooper and the rest went by way of Railroad Street, under constant fire from the bushes.

Halting near the drug store they fired upon the concealed enemies and wounded one Madden. Bud Tolliver was here shot in the thigh. Cal and Cate, who were mere boys, assisted Bud up the lane and secreted him in the weeds back of Johnson's store. They then rejoined their comrades. Cooper presently emerged from the Central Hotel and fired upon some of the Logan men, but was him shot through the breast. He retreated into the hotel and secreted himself in a wardrobe, upstairs, and in this place of fancied security was again hit by a bullet and killed.

The Central Hotel was surrounded, a cessation of firing ordered and Logan called upon the Tollivers to "come out and they should not be hurt." A woman delivered a message of the same purport to the Tollivers. She returned with Cate Tolliver, a boy fifteen years of age, who was disarmed and allowed to go unharmed. The others in the house refusing to surrender, Logan resorted to the tactics employed by the Tollivers against his cousins and directed his men to fire the building. The Tollivers broke cover and started for the bushes. Before leaving the house Craig Tolliver coolly pulled off his boots, saying that it had always been prophesied he would die with his boots on, and that he intended to disappoint the prophets. He emerged in his stocking feet.

Jay Tolliver got out the rear way, ran about fifty feet, was shot three times and fell dead. Craig and Andy broke from the hotel on the south side and were greeted with a hail of bullets. Andy was wounded twice, but not seriously, and under cover of the smoke succeeded in reaching the woods. Craig Tolliver's former good luck at last deserted him. He ran, firing at his enemies, down a lane, which leads from the hotel to the railroad track. At the corner of the drug store already spoken of, Pigman, Apperson Perry and three others were posted. They instantly opened fire on Tolliver, the score or more still at the hotel, also continuing their fusillade upon the fleeing outlaw.

Craig Tolliver ran a few steps beyond the corner of the store, fell, rose again and, running toward the switch, sank to the ground to rise no more. He was riddled with balls and buckshot. To the great regret of the Logan men, the man whose death they most desired, was not injured. This man was Bunk Mannin, the town marshal, who so brutally maltreated the dead bodies of the two Logan boys. There were undoubtedly some bad men in this fight against the Tollivers to whom may be ascribed some excesses which occurred on that memorable day. But they do not appear to have been actually connected with the Logan's. One of these men admitted that he fired three shots into the body of Jay Tolliver after he was down. This same man afterwards became a willing witness for the prosecution against the slayers of the Tollivers. It was this band of guerillas that shot Cooper while secreted in the hotel, dying from a wound in the breast. After completing their inhuman butchery, this same guerilla band sacked the American Hotel and committed other outrages.

The firing was continuous for two hours, except while the Logan's made proposals to the Tollivers to come out and surrender. Over fifteen hundred shots were fired. There was a general sense of relief among the inhabitants when the battle was over and the dreaded Tollivers were wiped out.

A public meeting was held and largely attended. A party, styling itself the Law and Order League, took possession of the town and held it until the arrival of troops. Boone Logan had faithfully kept his word and retaken his fireside. The sinking sun witnessed his return to the home from which he had been banished. His enemies had crossed over the great divide. For the first time in many months the town was quiet. The yells and defiant curses of the drunken desperadoes were heard no more. The lips that had uttered them were still. Peace entered Morehead once more. It has been purchased at the price of much blood.

The battle of June 22nd, 1887, was the last bloody clash between the various factions of Rowan County. The Tollivers, deprived of their leader, gave the town a wide berth after this. It soon resumed its former appearance of thrift and prosperity. Many of those who had removed from the county now returned and took possession of their abandoned property. Business houses, closed for many months, were reopened, the illegal saloons closed tight, and law and order have been reasonably well maintained in the county ever since.

Several of the Logan men were indicted for murder, Hiram M. Pigman, who had been Logan's right hand man, and of whom the latter spoke as the bravest and most circumspect man on the field that day, was indicted jointly with Apperson Perry. They were tried by a jury of Fleming County and promptly acquitted. Logan was never tried." The court was held under the protection of State troops. The trial lasted for seven days. Pigman and Perry were shown to be men of excellent character, neither of them had been parties to previous killings in Rowan County.

The evidence being concluded, the court instructed the jury. Briefly summarized, these instructions were 'Convict these defendants.' The jury, however, were really 'good men and true' and to the evident surprise of the court, and the chagrin of the prosecuting attorney, returned a verdict of not guilty. These jurymen had been summoned from the adjoining county of Fleming. Their names deserve the thanks of all good citizens of the Commonwealth. Obedience to the law and protection from the law, are reciprocal rights and duties, and this jury really decided that where those to whom it is delegated to administer the laws, and to protect the lives, liberty and property of the citizens, willfully disregard, or timidly refrain from discharging their duties, the citizen has the right to protect and defend himself." (Capt. McPherson's re port. Documents 1887. No. 23.).

The glaring partiality of the court and corruption of most of its officers he illustrates in the following language: "Not infrequently a witness would apply to an attorney the epithet of liar, and when questioned relative to some crime charged against him, a witness would defend his credibility on the ground that his questioner was guilty of offenses similar in character, which he would proceed to enumerate."Even the court would express his opinion in words of abuse and very plainly exhibited his partiality or prejudice.

Indeed, when the case of the Commonwealth against John Keeton was called for trial, and the affidavit of the defendant and two reputable housekeepers, asserting the belief that the presiding judge would not afford the defendant a fair and impartial trial was by the defendant handed to the judge, he remarked, after reading the instrument aloud, that he was not surprised; that John Keeton would swear anything; that he had sworn to so many lies already that it was not astonishing that he (the judge) would not give him a fair trial.

This observation of His Honor was delivered in the presence of the jury selected to try John Keeton." Reverting to the excesses committed by the guerillas during the battle and afterwards, Adjutant General Hill says: (Documents, Ky. 1887). "Almost every one with whom I talked, heartily approved the day's work, barring some excesses, which were committed, such as the killing of the two wounded men after the fight was over, and the disposition on the part of certain members of the posse to abuse their victory by manifesting some disregard of property rights, which conduct was bitterly lamented by the more conservative members of the posse, notably Boone Logan himself.

The victors of the 22nd of June were in the main, singularly moderate and forbearing, and it is denied by none of the people there that they rendered a most valuable service to the county in overthrowing the outlaws who had so long terrorized the community." During Circuit Court the commanding officers of the troops noticed one of the sheriffs and several Tolliver sympathizers in secret consultations. So suspicious were their actions that they were watched. In the afternoon these parties disappeared from Morehead. The next afternoon they brought a box of Springfield rifles, caliber fifty, by train.

One thousand rounds of ammunition accompanied the guns. Col. McKee promptly seized the arms over the vigorous protest of the Tolliver faction. The court had directed their shipment "for the purpose of securing peace and quiet and preventing a fight among citizens of this community. " Another order of the court declared "arms and weapons are kept or hidden or concealed, with the intent and purpose of being used by partisans of the factional war or strife now disturbing the peace, quiet and good order of said county of Rowan or being delivered to said partisans" etc., and directed the seizure of all arms. The officers complied, collecting all arms discovered in the possession of the Logan faction, and, of course, retaining the box of Springfield's consigned with White, a Tolliver sympathizer.

Then, strange to say, on August 24th, an order was issued by the Circuit Court directing the Colonel commanding the troops, or rather the Adjutant General, to immediately deliver to the sheriff the box of Springfield's and ammunition to arm a posse of citizens of Rowan County to make an arrest, and demanding a reply in writing should the officer refuse to comply with this strange order. The Adjutant General replied that he could not comply with the order for the reason that the arms could not be released except under direction from the Governor. The effect of obedience to this order would have been to restore the arms to the Tolliver faction, while retaining those of the Logan party, and to arm a posse, perhaps to be guided by Deputy Sheriff Hogg, with its recent infamous history still in mind, would scarcely have been consistent with the duty of an officer sent to Rowan County to preserve peace.

A day or two afterwards the court severely censured the Governor for not permitting His Honor to arm such sheriff's posse as he might select. Before departure from Rowan the officer commanding restored the guns and pistols taken from private individuals during the term of court. The box of Springfield rifles was retained and loaded upon the cars for shipment to Frankfort. The Tollivers were incensed. Deputy Sheriff Hogg and Andy White sauntered through town breathing threats and dire vengeance if the guns were not left behind.

The soldiers loading them, however, were not disturbed, and the guns were deposited in the arsenal at Frankfort. The presiding Circuit judge was soon afterwards, the following January, brought before the Legislature on impeachment proceedings. During the long-drawn out investigation many witnesses were examined, whose testimony fills an entire volume?

The result of the investigation was censure, a quasi whitewash, and a recommendation to abolish the county and attach it to another. But this would have meant nothing neither more nor less than to saddle upon innocent people the settlement of a controversy. To transfer the county to another district would have resulted in involving other sections hitherto not affected by the trouble. To abolish the county would have been an open acknowledgment of the weakness of the State to execute its laws and to cope with crime.

It was this confidence of the lawbreakers that their crimes would never be punished, and the belief of many good citizens that the machinery of the law was set in motion only in the interests of certain parties, that was responsible for the long continued, shameful disorders in Rowan County.

The End

Chapter Forty Five
Bad John Wright

This is taken from the" Courier Journal, an article by Joe Creason."

All that I know of Bad John Wright is what I have heard in Southeastern Kentucky. I have a feeling he is the most unusual Kentuckian of all.

John Wright lived in a remote corner of Letcher County is what today is Jenkins. It was him, the author John Fox Jr. used as a model for his character, Devil Jud Tolliver, in the book "Trail of the Lonesome Pine."

The mountain area around still abounds in John Wright tales. After the Civil Was, one hears he served as a peace officer and later worked as a land agent when John C.C. Mayo was acquiring the acreage, which became the vast holdings of The Consolidated Coal Company. As a peace officer, Wright engaged in many a shoot out; actually, one story holds that his greatest regret is that he never quite broke even in his life, what with having sired 27 children, but having killed 28 men in gun battles. Old timers recall hearing him tell about going once to serve a warrant on a notorious man who vowed that he would never be arrested. He was sitting in the front room that he remembered. Wright said, "When I talked in, he did not say anything, just whipped out his pistol and snapped the hammer down on the empty chamber. By then, I was getting somewhat nervous, of course, so I yanked out my pistol and shot him. If that taught me anything, it was to never let any man get the draw on me."

Bad John Wright owned and operated the sawmill at the foot of this hollow and the lumber from this plant was used to build the houses that are now in Wright's Hollow.

The author of this history spent much time with John W. Wright after he settled on Pound River to live out the declining days of his life. John Wright loved and always kept good horses. He became such an expert rider that the John Robinson Show hired him to ride for them before their great crowds. It was the fearless Devil John who made it possible more than a few times for circuit courts to convene in the mountains of Eastern Kentucky during the dangerous feud. Sometimes the judge who did not meet with the approval of the feuding tribe was routed from his bench, but when Devil John said, "Go ahead with your court, I will be hanging around," procedure took a different course. Devil John, who wanted his neighbors to do the right thing, and would have the right thing done if it required bullets, reconciled many a brawl that rose between coal operators and the citizens when Eastern Kentucky began to him with activity.

It was this self-made man whom John Fox depicted in the "Trail of the Lonesome Pine" and Devil Jud Tolliver. Bad John was asked it Fox ever came to see him. "Many times," he answered, glanced at me and then away at the distant hills. I suppose you knew quite well the Red Fox, I went on. "Yes," he answered, "Doc Taylor was a well known character. He was cunning, you never knew what to expect from him. "About how many men have you killed outside of the war?" I asked. "Seven" he replied positively, his keen eyes peering at me through his spectacles. He can see only out of the right eye' the left having been shot out by an adversary years ago. Some killings had to be done in those terrible days just after the war. There were too man horse thief's and murderers. However, I always gave a man the chance. Many times, I was shot at before I raised my gun. I suppose you practice shooting a great deal. "Everyday", I got so I raced my horse, would swing under his neck, shoot three times in rapid succession and I was coming to the cop, place a bullet in the center of the tree along the road. How many guns did you carry? "Just one, no use for more because by the time one was empty, I had my man or was ready to do something else". What kind of gun did you carry? "Usually a 38, sometimes I carried my war gun which was a 34." He stated he got his gun off a dead man on the banks of the Mississippi River. "I saw the man could not very well use it, and I needed it badly, and sir, she went on through the Civil War with me. Through several battles with the Indians in the West, also."

Devil John was Justice of the Peace for 16 years in the Eastern Hills of Kentucky and was sheriff for 8 years. For 30 years, he was a detective working in Virginia, West Virginia, and Kentucky. Outside of the war, did you kill anyone before you became a detective, I asked? "One he said, I went with a high sheriff and his deputy to capture a man in West Virginia, a horse thief. The sheriff and his deputy boldly approached and busted in without using any tact. I was bringing up the rear, bank, bank, and two officers fell as I entered the door, bank, a ball splintered the door facing right close to my head. Then in a flash I shot a bullet in the bed in the opposite side of the room, no shot returned. Three dead men lay still in the cabin. I went outside, jumped on my horse, and went to tell the people of the community what had happened."

"After a few years, I helped trace some rascals, and somehow my name began to be known far and near. A detective agency near Richmond, Virginia offered me a job and I accepted. I worked for them some time until they treated me dirty, and I offered my resignation. They said they would not accept it. I got out my old gun and said; "Guess I'll resign the agency then." Moreover, they seemed willing to let me go. The trouble was, they put me on the meanest, hardest cases and tried to keep all of the reward monies. However, straight away, offered me a job with the agency in Charleston, West Virginia, so I went.

"One hair raising adventure I had was one when I went with two county officers to capture a horse thief. He was a bad man; finally, I located him in a shoe shop. The officer that went with me took weak knees and would not go in with me. However, I went in, the man stooped over a bench in which lay a gun. My gun was in my pocket. I did not mean for him to take me as an officer and he did not until I said I want you. Then he flung his hand to his gun and shot twice. Luckily, he missed me. I did not have time to get my gun out, so I shot through my pocket and got him. Some of the people accused me of murdering the man and brought charges against me. Two men who were working in the shop swore that the thief shot himself. When I came to the stand, I explained just how it was and showed the hole in my trousers and was acquitted."

Chapter Forty-Six
They Built a Town

Jenkins is located at the foot of Pine Mountain in Letcher County, Kentucky. It is on the Sandy Valley and Elkhorn Railroad.

Consolidated Coal Company came into the mountains of Eastern Kentucky and built a city.

In the fall of 1911, the Consolidated Coal Company purchased one hundred thousand acres of coal lands in Pike, Letcher, and Floyd Counties, a part of the holdings of the Northern Coal and Coke Company that was gathered together during the previous ten years through the expenditure of much money and unbounded energy. Plans were made for the extension of the Lexington and Eastern Railroad from Jackson to a point on the north fork of the Kentucky River selected as the sight of a town, named McRoberts, in honor of Samuel McRoberts, vice-president of the City National Bank of New York and director of the Consolidated Coal Company. Plans were also made and a site selected for a town named Jenkins, in honor of George C. Jenkins, one of the leading citizens of Baltimore and a director of the Consolidated Coal Company.

To build the hundreds of homes and other structures needed, it was necessary to have a great deal of lumber, and the only way to get it was to cut down and saw up the trees that abounded on the company's land. Large quantities of brick were also needed. Therefore, nine saw mills, two, or three of them of the big band saw type, were hauled in, erected, and set to working. The machinery for two brickyards was also brought in and installed, as were steam and electric outfits for these and the temporary powerhouses. A temporary narrow-gauge railroad was built to carry on the work. This road from a connection at Glamorgan, Virginia was the Wise Terminal, a standard-gauge road and originally within eight miles of Jenkins. The Consolidated

Coal Company leased it, extended it three miles, and built a wagon road from its terminal five miles across the mountain to Jenkins. Over this mountain, then, were hauled on wagons the engines and boilers, and two narrow-gauge locomotives, saw mills and other mill equipment, the brick machinery, electric generators, logging outfits, and other things needed to carry on the work of building a town and mine opening. The heaviest things were twelve boilers, weighing 16,000 pounds each, one 40,000 and one 26,000-pound locomotives. It was necessary to hitch as many as twenty head of oxen to a wagon to haul one boiler. In addition, fool supplies had to be brought in. These tasks were accomplished in an incredibly short time, and when the railroad through Shelby Gap was completed to Jenkins, the Consolidated Coal Company was ready for business and had an output of several thousand tons of coal per day for shipment.

City Government was established in Jenkins only when Consolidated started selling the businesses and land to the people. Up until this time, Consolidated had hired its own marshals to enforce the law. Jenkins, was, however, established as a sixth-class town and was incorporated in 1912.

Jenkins is unique in its development as compared to other small towns because it did not come into existence by a small settlement over a period of years. Jenkins was planned, built for one purpose, which was to mine its coal, and for the men who came to operate it. With the opening of the mines, the nearest railroad was thirty miles distance. Consolidated therefore, undertook to build its own line, The Sandy Valley and Elkhorn Railroad. The construction of thirty miles of railroad began almost simultaneously with the opening, development and planning construction of 14 mines. The L & N Railroad with its nearest rails at Jackson, Kentucky, did not hesitate, after the development was assured, to build a line up the Kentucky River Valley in order to share in the transportation off what was to become known as the best quality coal in Kentucky.

Consolidated began its work on the construction of Jenkins. No one knows if the town was planned this way, but Jenkins is made up of four smaller towns. The towns incorporated under one small township were Dunham, Burdine, Jenkins, and up until a few years ago, McRoberts. When you speak of Jenkins, you speak of all of them. Each section was built separately. Times were good in the early twenties and thirties. At one time, Jenkins reached its peak in population with almost 10,000 people living within its city limits.

The biggest single social change in Jenkins came in early 1947 when Consolidated announced that the whole town of Jenkins was on the market. The following might explain this situation.

When one obtained a job with Consolidated, the company gave him a home rent-free. They paid no electric bills, water bills, sewage bills, and got fuel for a very small fee. Of course, the wages were small, but there was no sizeable outlay either. Part of the wages was paid in script. Script was a type of money printed by the company and could only be spend in company owned businesses. There was a company owned store, and the saying, "I owe my soul to the company store" started out this way.

It has been said, that the company brought the citizens of Jenkins into the world since they owned the only hospital, (where John Russell was born), and it escorted them out of this town since it owned the only funeral parlor.

4th of July celebrations included, climbing greasy poles, chasing pigs, people come from these mountains and hollows all around here. You wouldn't think they was that many people around, just all day long, boxing matches, races, baseball games, anything.

Remembering some of the good baseball players –

Bonnie Weaver was outstanding. He went to Washington. John Brooder with to Chicago and there was Jim Mooney. Bob Bowman went to St. Louis and was sold for $75000 from Chicago to St. Louis. Ray Russell now, he was a ball player. Yes, actually he was a professional ball player when he came to Jenkins. He could have been in the big leagues if he would have gone. Ray was outstanding and Sam Hancock was outstanding. Sam played outfield most of the time, and Ray was an outfielder. We had as many as 3000 people come to some of the games. People used to sit on the hillside and watch. They had baseball fields at Burdine, Dunham, and McRoberts. The field at Burdine was there about the Ashland Station and at Dunham, it was up there around Bad John Wright's place, and at McRoberts, it was where it is now. We had Grady Dobin, which were a first baseman and a long ball hitter. Monie Weaver, he went to the major leagues. We have had two or three fellows here that played ball and went to the major leagues, Wolf Pit, Hellier, and Burdine.

Like a still river that flows through the community and city, we remember the good it did for those who used it and benefited from its use, so do we want to remember those who made it a pleasant place to live and gave it character that we will remember today and all the days of our lives.

People stuck together better than in any part of the corporation. Such as in death when people helped to dig graves. There is something magical about Eastern Kentucky that keeps bringing people back. No one can put a finger on it. The mining cars were let down the hill by rope in 1912 to be dumped in coal cars.

Chapter Forty-Seven
History of Taillefer/Taliaferro/ Tolliver

St. Arnulf, Bishop of Metz (died 641), had a son Ansegisel, whose son Pepin of Harstal, (died 715) whose natural son Charles Martel, reigned 715-741, whose son Pepin 3rd, reigned 741-768, called Pepin the Short, King of the Franks, had a son called Charlemagne or Charles The Great, reigned 768-814, King of the Franks, Holy Roman Emperor, whose won was Louis the Pious, crowned King 816-840.

Centuries of history omitted from this narrative to give a simple overview. I strongly recommend that you read the history of the times these events took place to get a proper perspective and to put a foundation under the Tolliver family.

Guillaume D'Orange 750-812, was a leader of the armies of Charlemagne and a hero of a group of Southern French Chansons de Geste (epic French verse of the Middle Ages), who was born in what is now Northern France. He was known as Fierabrace, Saint Guillaume de Gellone, and Marquis Au Court Nez (Marquis Short Nose). His prowess as a soldier let Charlemagne to charge him with the training of his son, Louis the Pious (King Louis 1st), whose surname was Le Debonnaire.

King Louis 1st, Holy Roman Emperor, had a son by Judith, his second wife who was called King Charles le Chauve (Charles the balk), King of France from 840-977, and Holy Roman Emperor. In the year of our Lord 866, he created the independent country of Angouleme, and made Vulgrin, one of his relatives, the first Count of Angouleme. This was in the days of feudalism, or the feudal system, when the King would parcel out sections of his kingdom within itself, to others to rule for him. These sections given to others were knowns as "fiefs" or "feuds" (sometimes countries), and each fief was a kingdom within itself, responsible ONLY to the King.

Count Vulgrin 1st, reined 866-886, was the first of a long line of Norman Counts that extended into the 13th Century. Guillaume 1st, 3rd Count of Angouleme, reined 916-975, came by the name Taillefer (first of the name) as a result of a battle with a Norman Chief, Stonius. He is credited with, "during the battle he cleaved from head to foot the body and armor of Stonius." Taillefer, pronounced Tolliver, means cleaver or cutter of iron, and it the French spelling, and was spelled this way as long as French was the literary language of England. When English became the common language (Henry 4th), the name had been changed to the Latin spelling of Taliaferro.

Thus, when a Norman knight came to England with William the Conquerer, 1027-1087 (also a descendant of St. Arnulf) and took part in the Battle of Hastings in 1066, exhibiting great fighting ability with his sword, it was no surprise that his name was Taillefer.

Taillefer the surname of a bard and warrior of the 11th Century whose exact name and place of birth are unknown. He accompanied the Norman Army to England in 1066, and obtained permission from William to strike the first blow at the Battle of Hastings. He fought with spirit and determination and was killed in battle. "*This from the Encyclopedia Britannica, 11th Edition, Edition, Volume XXVI, page 3580*

Chapter Forty-Eight
Origin of the Taliaferro Name
Published Beliefs
And
Family Traditions

There are many branches of the Taliaferro name, each having their own beliefs and thoughts on where the name originated. Many of these stories have been in the family for so many years that they have become tradition, passed from one generation to the other.

There was a NORMAN KNIGHT, named TAILLEFER, who was HERO of "The Battle of Hastings"

The army got into action from the hills of Telman or Heathland, marching to attack the English on the opposite hills of Senlac. A Norman called Taillefer, "who sang very well, and rode a horse which was fast, came up to the Duke (William the Conqueror), Milord, I have served you long, and you owe me for all my services: pay me today, and if it pleases, grant unto me, for recompense in full, to strike the first blow in the battle." William granted this wish. "So Taillefer darted before him singing the deeds of Charlemagne, and of the vassals who fell at Roncesvalles. As he sang he played with his sword, throwing it into the air and catching it in his right hand, and the Normans followed, repeating the songs, crying, GOD HELP." *This was taken from "A Popular History of France, Volume 1, by M. Guizot"*

"A general charge of the Norman foot opened the battle (The Battle of Hastings). In front rode the minstrel Taillefer, tossing his sword in the air and catching it again while he chanted the songs of Roland. He was the first of the host who struck a blow, and the first to fall." *This was taken from "The History of the English People, page 145, by John Richard Green"*

"With the morning the Battle of Hastings opened, the battle that was to determine the fate of England. It was started by a horseman riding out from the Norman lines and advancing alone toward the English Army, tossing up his sword and skillfully catching it as it fell, and singing, all the while, the stirring battle-songs of Charlemagne and Roland. The English watched with astonishment this, careless dexterity, and if they did not construe the vivacity and nimbleness of the Norman foe with their own heavy and clumsy manners, others at least have not failed to do so for them." *This was taken from "Outlines of Medieval and Modern History, page 173, by V.N. Myers"*

In the middle of the Duke's cohort, was the sacred gonfalon, and in front of it wand of the whole line, rode a strange warrior of gigantic height. As he rode the warrior sang and the knights, no longer singing hymn, swelled, hoarse through their helmets, the martial chorus. This warrior in front of the Duke and the horsemen seemed beside himself with the joy of the battle. As he rode, and as he chanted, he threw up his sword in the air like a gleeman, catching it nimbly as it fell, and flourishing it wildly, till, as if unable to restrain his fierce exhilaration, he fairly put spurs to his horse and, dashing forward to the very front of the detachment of Saxon riders, shouted 'A Taillefer, A Taillefer' and by voice and gesture challenged forth some to single combat.

A fiery your man who knew the Romance tongue, started forth and crossed swords with the poet, but by what seemed rather a sleight of hand than a knights fair fence, Taillefer, again throwing up and catching his sword with incredible rapidity, shore the unhappy Saxon from helm to the chine, and riding over the corpse, shouting and laughing, he again renewed his challenge. A second rode forth and shared the same fate. The rest of the English horsemen stared at each other in awe, the shouting, singing, juggling giant seemed to then not knight, but demon, and that single incident preliminary to all other battle, in sight of the whole field, might have sufficed to damp the ardor of the English, had not Leofwine, who had been dispatched by the King with a message to the entrenchments, came in front of the detachment, and his gay spirit rose and stung by the insolence of the Norman, and the evident dismay of the Saxon riders, without thought of his graver duties, he spurred his steed to the Norman giant, and not even drawing his sword, but with his spear raised over his head, and his form covered by his shield, he cried in the Romance of his native tongue. "Go and chant to the foul fiend" Taillefer rushed forward, his sword shivered on the Saxon shield, and in the same moment he fell a corpse under the hoofs of his steed, transfixed by the Saxon spear." *This was taken from the book "Harold, the Last of the Saxon Kings, by Edward Lytton"*

Chapter Forty-Nine
The Counts of Angouleme - *And Isabelle Taillefer*

"Angouleme, a city located in Southwest France, was taken by Clovis, from the Visigoths in 507 and plundered by the Normans in the 9th century. In 1360 it was surrendered by the peace of Brittany to the English. They were expelled in 1373 by the troops of Charles V, who granted the town numerous privileges. It suffered much during the Wars of Religion, especially in 1568 after its capture by the Protestants under Colony. The Counts of Angouleme date from the 9th century, the most important of the early Counts being WILLIAM TAILLEFER, whose descendants held the title until the end of the 12th century. Withdrawn from them on more than one occasion by Richard-de-Lion, it passed to King John, of England, on his marriage with Isabelle, daughter of Count Ademar, and by her subsequent marriages, in 1220, to Hugh X passed to the Lusignan, Counts of Marche." *This was taken from the "Encyclopedia Britannica, 11th edition, Volume 2, pages 41-42"*

"The legend which accounts for the origin of the Taillefer name in France is given by the chronicler Amimer de Chabanois, who related that in the 10th century, William, Count of Angouleme, (grandson of Wulgrin, the first Count and Kinsman of Charles the Bald) assumed the name of Taillefer after having defeated Storis (Stonius), a King of the Northmen, in single combat, the reason for his doing so being that he had performed the great knightly achievement of hewing his adversary literally in twain, through the breastplate and breastbone, with one single stroke of his good sharp sword." *This was taken from the book of "Borlace of Borlace by William Copeland Borlase, 1888*

Chapter Fifty
A Brief Sketch of the *Counts of Angouleme*

1. Rogelinde of Poitiers, married Vulgrin I, died 886. The first hereditary Count of Angouleme. Reigned 866-886.
2. Andoinn 2nd Count of Angouleme. Reigned 886-916.
3. Guillaume I, 3rd Count of Angouleme, called Taillefer, Cleavor of Iron, because during battle "with a terrific blow of his sword, he cleaved into, from head to feet, the body and armor of Stonius, a Norman chief, thereby terminating the Norman invasions of this region." He transmitted the Taillefer name to all his posterity, died 975, and reigned 916-975. (This is the same Count that is previously mentioned as William, Count of Angouleme).
4. Amand Taillerfer, 4th Count of Angouleme, married Hildegarde.
5. Guillaume Taillefer II, 5th Count of Angouleme, reined 1001-1028, was the builder of the Cathedral of Angouleme, the builder of the Palace that was later known as Maison Taillefer, where Queen Elizabeth of England was born. He married Gerberge d'Anjou, the daughter of Geoffrey Grisonelle, Count of Anjou.
6. No information, reigned 1028-1030
7. Geoffrey Taillefer, 7th Count of Angouleme, reined 1030-1-48, married Petron d'Archiac, died 1048.
8. Fulk Taillefer, 8th Count of Angouleme, reined 1048-1108, married Coude, daughter of Ournorman Vagaua.
9. Guillaume Taillefer III, 9th Count of Angouleme, reigned 1108-1120, webnt to the Holy Land with a company if Knights, died on the return

trip. Married Corlieu de Vitapoi, daughter of Amanieu.

10. Vulgrin Taillefer II, 10th Count of Angouleme, reigned 1120-1140, born 1099, died 1140.
11. Guillaume Tallefer IV, 11th Count of Angouleme, reined 1140-1178, died at Messina on his way to the Holy Land in 1178. Married 1136 to Emme de Limoges "after he kidnapped her from her affianced husband, William X, Duke of Auitaine. She was the daughter of Aymer IC, Vicomte of Limoges. They had three sons who were successively Counts of Angouleme."
12. Vulgrin Tallifer III, 12 th Count of Angouleme, his reign started 1178, he abdicated in 1179, and died in 1181. His only child, Mathilde Taillefer, died 1233. Countess of La Marche in her own right after her cousin, Aldebert de Montgomery V, Count of Le Marche died with out issue in 1180. She married Hugh de Lusignan, Count of La Marche. Mathidle betrothed her infant son, Hugh de Lusignan X, to her infant first cousin, Isabelle Taillefer, in the desire to bring together again the rich estates of the two branches of the Taillefer family. Thus, as was the custom, Isabelle was taken to the Lusignan castle so Mathilde might rear and educate her successor and as a virtuous wife for her son. In French records and history evidence that Mathilde's efforts were successful, for Isabelle was known in her native land to have been one of the most refined, pious and splendidly educated of the noble heiresses of that period.
13. Guillaume Taillefer V, 13th Count of Angouleme, reined 1180-1185, died without issue in 1185, was succeeded by his younger brother.
14. Aymer Taillefer, 14th Count of Angouleme, reined 1185-1217, died 1217 and was buried in Chapelle St. Nicholas La Couronne near Angoulene, one of the churches built and endowed by his daughter, the Countess – Queen, as Isabelle chose to call herself after her 2nd marriage. Aymer Taillefer's only child and heiress was Isabelle Taillefer. Isabelle, as stated above, was betrothed, while still in infancy, to her infant cousin, Hugh de Lusignan (Hugh the X). Many things were destined to happen before this wedding was to take place. While Isabelle Taillefer did, eventually marry Hugh X she was first to marry King John of England. *This information was based on the book "Magna Carta by John S Wurts"*

Chapter Fifty One
Isabelle Taillefer and King John of England

King John of England (the brother of Richard Coeur de Lion) was the hated John of the Robin Hood legends, the John whom his rebellious Barons forced to sign the famous Magna Carta (The Great Charter) on June 15, 1215. King John, divorced from his first wife, attended the announced wedding of Isabelle Taillefer and Hugh X at St. Cybard Abbey, near Angouleme on August 26, 1200. King John was so taken with the beauty of the bride to be, that he compelled the Bishop of Angouleme, Jean de St. Val, to celebrate his own marriage with Isabelle in the church where already people were assembled for the ceremony between Isabelle and Hugh. Then, after the marriage had been performed, King John took his stolen bride to Bordeaux, where his own Archbishop of Bordeaux solemnly declared that no impediments existed to the marriage, and again united their hands in the marriage rites.

This threw Count Hugh X, the husband to be, into despair and he challenged to mortal combat the royal interloper. The wily John answered to the effect that if Count Hugh wished for combat he would appoint a champion to fight with him. Unable to obtain satisfaction from King John, Hugh X, with Isabelle's father, Aymer Taillefer appealed to King Philip of France for redress, while King John sailed with his unhappy bride for England.

When King John and his stolen bride arrived in England, he called a council of the Kingdom at Westminster, where Isabelle was introduced and acknowledged as Queen-Consort of England. There exists a charter in the Tower of London, stating that Isabelle Taillefer, of Angouleme, was crowned

Queen by the common consent of the Barons, Clergy, and the people of England at Westminster, 8th October 1200, by Hubert Walter, Archbishop of Canterbury.

Isabelle intrigued constantly and contrived to install her relatives in the majority of the most lucrative posts in England. These relatives were probably members of the Lusignan and La Marche clans as well as the Taillefers.

When King John died in 1216, Isabelle, his widow, then returned to France and there she married Hugh X, whom she was preparing to marry at the time she was stolen by King John. Many of the Taillefer relatives, who had followed her to England, remained and established families in England.

Isabelle Taillefer, of Angouleme, born August 26, 1186 at the Manson Taillefer at Angouleme, Charente, France, died 1246, and was buried at Fontevrault Abbey, Main-et-Loire, where her remarkable tomb of sculpture and painted oak yet remains. This sculptured image is believed to be her best likeness as it was commissioned and placed in the Royal Chapel by her son, Henry III, King of England, at the side of his grandparents, King Henry II and Eleanor of Aquitaine, and near his uncle, Richard Coeur-de-Lion. The latter three effigies are of sculptured stone. The British Government at one time tried to get permission to remove all four to Westminster Abbey, but the French government refused the request. *This information is based on the book "The Pageantry of England by Costain"*

Chapter Fifty Two
The Barbarian *and* Julius Caesar

About 58 B.C. Julius Caesar, while on a campaign in Northern Gaul, was making an inspection of his camp and became separated from his men. Before Caesar could find his way back to his men he became surrounded by a band of barbarians and while fighting for his life, showed such courage in the fight, of which he has not a chance to win, that the leader of the barbarians so admired the courage of Caesar that he stopped the fight and spared the life of Caesar.

Caesar then rewarded the barbarian, who had saved his life, by taking him into the Roman camp, which was an honor, as the Romans did not permit outsiders to enter their camps. In time the barbarian was made the personal arms bearer for Caesar and was given the name Tailefer that, it is said, came from the Latin words "Tatum," meaning a dart, or spear, and "Ferre," meaning to bear. It is from this barbarian, know as "Tailefer, that the Italian family Tagliaferro is supposed to have been derived. *This is taken from "An Old Family Legend."*

Chapter Fifty-Three
Bartholomew Taliaferro of England

1. BARTHOLOMEW TALIAFERRO, d. September 22, 1601, buried at St. Olave's, Hart Street, London, England. w. Joane Lane, m. January 1, 1583/4 at St. Michael's, Cornhill, London, England. Joane Lane m. (2) Thomas Graye of Whitechapel County, Middlesex on May 15, 1602, d. June 12, 1617.

- i. KATHERINE, b. Nov. 29, 1584, d. Jan. 12, 1584/85
- ii. HORATIO, b. Jan. 16, 1585/86, d. July 21, 1593
- iii. SIPRION, b. Feb. 25, 1587/88, d. Sept. 7, 1609 b. St. Bishopsgate, London, England.
- iv. FRANCIS, b. Jan 25, 1589/90
- v. IZACK (twin), b. March 18, 1592, d. Aug. 2, 1610
- vi. JACOB (twin), b. March 18, 1592, d. Aug 2, 1593
- vii. ELYZABETH, b. Jan 25, 1594/95, m. Feb. 27, 1611/12 stepbrother William Graye d., 1617, stepfather, Thomas Graye.
- viii. BARTHOLOMEW, b. Dec 9, 1596, d. Dec. 10, 1596
- viii. JEROMME, b. 1598, d. 1609, age 11

2. FRANCIS TALIAFERRO [1.iv], male, (Bartholomew Taliaferro[1]) born Bethnal Green, Stepney, Middlesex County, b. Jan. 25, 1589/90, d. Aug. 19, 1647, m. (1) Bennett Hale, Feb., 3, 1613/14. m (2) Mariam

Children by Bennett Hale:

i. Anne

ii. Robert, b. Nov. 19, 1626

3. ROBERT TALIAFERRO [2.ii,] male (Francis Taliaferro [1iv], Bartholomew Taliaferro[1]) b. Nov 19, 1626, IMMIGRANT from England to Virginia at age 8. (First of the Taliaferro name to reach America).

i. FRANCIS, of Gloucester County, Virginia, was a Gentleman. Made grats to his brothers on September 18, 1682 from the lands granted to their father, jointly owned with Lawrence Smith on March 26, 1666 in Rappahannock (later became Caroline and Spotsylvania County, Virginia).

ii. JOHN, m. Sarah Smith, daughter of Lawrence Smith

iii. RICHARD

iv. CHARLES

Chapter Fifty Four
John Taliaferro Toliver

Revolutionary War pension application affidavits state that John, Moses, and Jesse were definitely brothers. Jesse was born on the Rappahannock River in Prince William County, VA. By the time John was born, that area had become Fauquier County. Shortly afterward, the family moved to the James River area about 30 miles from Richmond. Information in John's military pension file and that of this brother Jesse indicated that they are their brother Moses, (there may have been two other brothers, Charles and William), came to NC with their father before the Revolutionary War began. The identity of their father has not been definitely proven, but it is likely that his name was either John or William, since those are the only two Toliver males who appear on tax lists of the correct period. Further, about five or six years before the Revolutionary War began (about 1770) the family moved to Surry (later Wilkes) County, NC east of the Blue Ridge Mountains. The father was still living and was involved in this move, but he is not named in any of the pension records of Jesse or John. Land records show Tollivers buying extensively along the Roaring River, Mulberry Creek, and the Yadkin River between 1778 and 1781. Following the Battle of King's Mountain (1780s) the Tolliver brother and other in the family including their mother (who is not named) moved west of the Blue Ridge to the part of Wilkes that later became Ashe and still later became Ashe and still later became Alleghany County. There was no mention of the father being involved in the 1780 move. If William Toliver (1730-1774) was the father of Moses, Jesse, John, and some or all of the others, his death in 1774 fits the fact of the absence of the father in 1780. In addition, there is a William Toliver on tax lists in Surry County in 1771 and 1772 (Wilkes was formed from Surry in 1777). Of course, to "muddy the waters" a bit, there is also a John Toliver there during the same years.

Chapter Fifty Five
John Oxford

Oxford takes, "one day at a time".
Former Miner didn't retire until age 90.

It was an unusually busy week at the Heritage Hall Nursing Home as about 40 people visited one resident.

John Oxford was getting the attention as he prepared to celebrate his 100th birthday, January 29th.

Nobody enjoyed himself more than Oxford, a lively participant in party banter as cake and all the trimmings were served.

Oxford appeared most content with his first six months' residence at the "nourishment home," his descriptive alternative for a nursing home. Three squares a day, served piping hot, with good company just down the hall helped compensate for the sacrifice of a little independence, he conceded.

Independence was an attribute Oxford has protected fiercely until last July when he enter the facility.

"I went to visit him a couple of years ago, and couldn't find him in the house," his nephew Jim Oxford recalled. "John was up on the roof making what he called a few little repairs. Although he barely weighed 90 pounds himself, he has somehow hauled 90 pound rolls of tarpaper up a ladder, unrolled it, and was tacking it down. He'd taken the precaution of tying himself to the chimney with a piece of rope in case he slipped, and had used a 2x4 to keep the tarpaper aligned on the roof."

The elder Oxford only grins as such stories are told.

Life, he said, has been good to him and he's always found something in each day, no matter how hard, to look forward to.

Oxford was the fourth of nine children born to James Oliver Oxford and Liddie Collinsworth Oxford at this grandfather's farm about two miles from Jonesville. His grandfather, William Oxford, had settled in the area more than a decade before the Civil War.

He recalled his boyhood home clearly. He remembered watching his father born and scrapes empty 60-gallon wooden barrels used to ship kerosene so they could be used to store food the family preserved.

"We'd put up a barrel each of pickled beans, corn and kraut and two or three of molasses," he said. And then there would be dried apples, pumpkin, peaches, berried, beans and cushaw to cook through the winter, he added.

Sweet potatoes were taken to a cave adjoining the old home place, a cave that stayed relatively dry and warm every winter.

Hogs were permitted to run wild, each marked with the owner's distinctive ear clipping signature to help identify property when slaughtering time came. And there always seemed to be a gang of chickens going around behind the hogs, picking up leftovers, he said, grinning.

Walking about 2 ½ miles to a one-roomed school was a daily ritual for him six months out of each year from first through fifth grades. But then there was work to be done elsewhere and school was behind him.

The family farm contained Oxford Ford, a popular river crossing point for travelers going between Wallens Creek and Jonesville.

"There were few ferries used back then. People looked for a shallow place to ford the river and drove their horses or mules across," he recalled, adding that there were no bridges back then.

He recalled childhood visitors to Jonesville where chain gangs, prisoners from area jails, were assigned to break up rocks for use in paving the dirt streets. They were often seen out dragging their heavy ball and chain restraints as they moved about doing their work. And hitching posts, later to be replaced by motor meters, provided places for shoppers to park their vehicles.

He learned the importance of earning an income early in life. Pairing with another boy, he would hire out as a "team" to dig potatoes, hoe corn or mow wheat by hand, the two youngsters splitting the wages of an adult worker, about 50 cents a day.

He also learned early to hunt and trap, becoming adept at catching possums, pole cats, rabbit, mink, coon and muskrats to sell for hides. A black pole cat hide brought from $3 to $5, depending on the condition of the pelt that season. But a mink was always good for about $7.

"First suit I ever bought me got buried on account of a black pole cat," he recalled, laughing. "I and my brother went out to check traps on Sunday morning before church and I had that new suit on. I went way around that trap, around by an old tree to stay clear of it, but that pole cat was hard to handle. When I went up to try and help my brother, that thing flipped around and got me good. He had a few white hairs on his tail, but we felt justified plucking them out to sell him for black after what he cost me."

When he was 15 years old, he began working in the burgeoning logging industry to the area. His job was to make the logs into rafts for the long trip down river to markets in Chattanooga, Tennessee.

Rafts were lashed and pegged together, each manned for the trip down the Powell River. Conditions bettered down river, where two rafts could be lashed together and part of the raft crew could walk home. By the time loggers reached the Little Tennessee River, four rafts could be lashed together for the remaining leg of the trip.

"All the boys who worked logging would generally walk back home, even from Chattanooga, a fellow made 50 cents a day getting the logs down river. It didn't make much sense to pay the railroad 50 cents to get back home when the walk only took two or three days."

The family moved to the Keokee area long before rumors of trouble in Europe made Americans worry about the specter of what would later become World War I.

Jobs on the railroad, a stint as owner/operator of a Millstone, Ky. Club house where migrant coal miners lived, and working in coal mines kept John going. He worked in a total of ten mined in Virginia and ten in Kentucky during his lifetime.

John's father was killed by a train while driving his horse and wagon across a railroad crossing in Pardee in January of 1913, and his mother died in December of that year. He buried his parents in the cemetery at the head of Pardee and assumed responsibility for the care of his younger sisters while younger brothers Jim and Harve, then 15 and 16, went off to fight in France during World War I.

In the 1930s and 1940s, he built a home in the section of Big Stone Gap he called simply "the Bottom," and worked at construction of a garage, the building later occupied by Glenn Roberts Firestone. His first wife, Cindy Estep Oxford, ran a small grocery store in the town. They were married 35 years before she died.

He later married Leona Herron and the couple made their home in the Wildcat area, where they opened a small store which remained in operation until John "retired" at age 90.

In 1962, when he was just 71 years old, he made one more venture into coal mining. He had been a United Mine Workers activist and organizer during his career as an employee. But now, he would become a coal operator for six years.

"I bought 19 acres of coal, build me a little tipple and hired five or six men," he said. "I ran that for six years until the laws started changing and it just got to be too hard. I got out of it in 1988, when I was 77, and went back to just piddling around with the store."

Although he had no children, there were two stepsons and one stepdaughter, nine step grandchildren, about 50 nephews and nieces, more than 100 great nephews and nieces, and several "great-greats" he enjoyed sharing the past few decades with. Only his sister Pearl and three cousins, Frank, Maude and Ethel, survive from his immediate family.

Nephew Jim Oxford recalled a favorite "Uncle John" story which characterized the philosophy which led to a long life.

A battle with cancer under his uncle's left eye resulted in a series of radiation treatments and some time at the University of Virginia three years ado. Doctors, asking about medications the patient was taking, were astonished when the 97 year old replied, "Alka-seltzer, vitamins, a little baking soda if I need it bad enough."

"No blood pressure or heart medications, no special diet or other restrictions?

"No disrespect, but that stuff will kill you if you start on it," John replied. "I always did all right just working hard and taking one day at a time."

Chapter Fifty-Six
Descendants of William Oxford

Generation No. 1

1. WILLIAM1 OXFORD was born September 27, 1823 in Jonesville, Lee County, Virginia. He married EVALINE LAWSON September 26, 1850 in Lee, Virginia, daughter of R LAWSON and SARAH.

Notes for WILLIAM OXFORD:
Settled in the area more than a decade before the Civil War.
Quoted from his Grandson, John Green Oxford, Post Newspaper Article, Page 4, Wednesday, January 30, 1991
Burial place, Oxford Cemetery, Jonesville, Lee County, Virginia.
Frank Oxford signed Death Certificate.
Lived 76 years, 8 months and 5 days on this earth.
Cause of death was Congestive Heart Failure due to Arterovascular Heart Disease.
His occupation was a farmer.
Was preceded in death by his wife.

Children of WILLIAM OXFORD and EVALINE LAWSON are:

2 i. JAMES OLIVER2 OXFORD, b. February 06, 1861; d. January 12, 1914, Pardee, Virginia.

ii. ROSE ANNA OXFORD, b. February 10, 1867, Jonesville, Lee County, Virginia; d. August 18, 1935; m. ANDREW KILEANON BONHAM, July 27, 1893.

iii. JOHN OXFORD, b. December 19, 1855, Lee County, Virginia; m. ROSA

POTEET.

iv. SARAH OXFORD, b. June 09, 1853, Lee County, Virginia; m. GEORGE EDWARDS, November 30, 1876.

v. HANNAH JANE OXFORD, b. December 22, 1851; d. Unmarried.

vi. MARY A. OXFORD, b. May 24, 1858, Lee County, Virginia; d. Unmarried.

vii. LUCINDA OXFORD, b. February 25, 1863; m. WILLIAM H. COLLINSWORTH, March 15, 1896.

viii. MALANIE OXFORD, b. February 25, 1865; m. JAMES STANDIFER.

ix. WILLIAM GREEN OXFORD, b. February 17, 1869, Lee County, Virginia; d. October 22, 1945; m. LILLY MIZE.

Generation No. 2

2. JAMES OLIVER^2 OXFORD *(WILLIAM^1)* was born February 06, 1861, and died January 12, 1914 in Pardee, Virginia. He married LYDIA A. COLLINSWORTH October 25, 1883 in Jonesville, Lee County, Virginia.

Notes for JAMES OLIVER OXFORD:
Batch #8423404, Sheet 21, Source Call # 1395849
On January 12, 1914 was struck by a railway train accidental while crossing with a card.
James Ray Oxford Jr. had a picture drawn of this intersection as memorial tribute.
His occupation was a farmer.
Married at age 22 to L.A. Collinsworth age 19
Notes for LYDIA A. COLLINSWORTH:
Liddie Oxford is how she signed her name on Death Certificate of James Oliver Oxford.
She lived to be 50 years old, occupation listed as housewife.
She died of Chronic Blights Disease, Chronic Interstitial Nephritis, and Kidney Failure, which lasted for one year.

Children of JAMES OXFORD and LYDIA COLLINSWORTH are:

3. i. JAMES RAY^3 OXFORD, SR, b. March 10, 1898, Keokee, Virginia; d. February 18, 1968.

ii. HARVE MARION OXFORD, b. March 30, 1895; d. February 03, 1964.

iii. JOHN GREEN OXFORD, b. January 29, 1891; d. June 10, 1993, Big Stone Gap, Virginia.

Notes for JOHN GREEN OXFORD:
The family farm contained Oxford Ford, a popular river crossing point for travelers going between Wallens Creek and Jonesville.

4. iv. SAMUEL OXFORD.

v. MORGAN OXFORD.

vi. SARA OXFORD.

vii. PEARL OXFORD, b. May 22, 1904; d. February 20, 1992.

viii. ADDIE OXFORD.
ix. WILLIAM OXFORD, b. September 09, 1885, Lee County, Virginia.

Generation No. 3

3. JAMES RAY[3] OXFORD, SR *(JAMES OLIVER[2], WILLIAM[1])* was born March 10, 1898 in Keokee, Virginia, and died February 18, 1968. He married IDA PRISCILLA TOLLIVER, daughter of CHARLIE TOLLIVER and ELIZABETH (BENTLY). b. May 18, 1905, d. August 27, 1944. She had one brother named CALVIN TOLLIVER, who married MARY J. CRESS, October 6, 1859.

Notes for IDA PRISCILLA TOLLIVER:
Gravestone Inscription: Mother, Ida Tolliver Oxford, Born, May 18, 1905 – Died, August 27, 1944 "To Love is Still to Have", her son James R Oxford, Jr. had this stone put on the grave.
She died at age 39 from Pneumonia due to Crippling Arthritis.

Children of JAMES OXFORD and IDA TOLLIVER are:

5. i. GERALDINE[4] OXFORD, b. May 06, 1923.
6. ii. CHARLIES JACQUELINE OXFORD, b. September 09, 1931.
7. iii .GLORIA ANN OXFORD, b. January 26, 1934; d. November 29, 1980.
8. iv. MAGDALINE OXFORD, b. December 08, 1924.
9. v. BEATRICE LORINE OXFORD, b. May 01, 1926; d. December 20, 1971.
10. vi. JAMES RAY OXFORD JR., b. March 18, 1929.

4. SAMUEL[3] OXFORD *(JAMES OLIVER[2], WILLIAM[1])*.

Children of SAMUEL OXFORD are:

i. WILLIAM[4] OXFORD.
11. ii. PAUL OXFORD.
iii. ANNA LOU OXFORD, m. (UNKNOWN) DREARY, Dryden, Virginia.
iv. VIRGINIA OXFORD, m. (UNKNOWN) ESTEP, Kingsport, Va.
v. MYRTLE OXFORD, m. (UNKNOWN) GOINS, Kingsport, TN.
vi. FAYE OXFORD, m. MORRIS ESTEP, Big Stone Gap, VA.
vii. IDA BELLE OXFORD, m. (UNKNOWN) DREARY, Pennington Gap, Virginia.
viii. LILLIE MAE OXFORD, m. (UNKNOWN) BLEDSOE, Pennington Gap, Virginia.

Generation No. 4

5. GERALDINE[4] OXFORD *(JAMES RAY[3], JAMES OLIVER[2], WILLIAM[1])* was born May 06, 1923. She married July 19, 1941 son of JESS MOREFIELD and DORA

HAMMONDS (1) CLARENCE KING MOREFIELD SR. born November 4, 1918 in Rowdy, Virginia and he died September 16, 1989 and she married (2) RICHARD PONTO January 17, 1969 in Monroe, Mi.

Children of GERALDINE OXFORD and CLARENCE SR are:

12. i. SHARON KAY5 MOREFIELD, b. September 19, 1957, Detroit, MI.
13. ii. CLARENCE KING MOREFIELD JR, b. February 13, 1944, Idaho.
14. iii. JOHN RUSSELL MOREFIELD, b. August 26, 1946, Jenkins, Kentucky.

6. CHARLIES JACQUELINE[4] OXFORD was born September 9, 1931 and she died September 7, 2007.

7. GLORIA ANN[4] OXFORD *(JAMES RAY[3], JAMES OLIVER[2], WILLIAM[1])* was born January 26, 1934, and died November 29, 1980. She married MACK JOHN STAJDA on August 12, 1961, born October 28, 1918 he died and was buried in Michigan Memorial Cemetery in Flatrock, MI.

Children of GLORIA OXFORD and MACK STAJDA are:

i. GREGORY ALLAN[5] STAJDA, b. May 05, 1954 adopted by Mack John Stajda.
ii. MARY ANN STAJDA, b. February 05, 1962 born Detroit, MI
15. iii. CONSTANCE STAJDA, b. November 22, 1963 born Detroit, MI

8. MAGDALINE[4] OXFORD *(JAMES RAY[3], JAMES OLIVER[2], WILLIAM[1])* was born December 08, 1924. She married ALBERT (ELMER RAY) JOHNSON, and they had 12 children.

9. BEATRICE LORINE[4] OXFORD *(JAMES RAY[3], JAMES OLIVER[2], WILLIAM[1])* was born May 01, 1926, and died December 20, 1971. She married HERBERT WINCHELL born May 18, 1944, and died about 1977 or 1978.

Children of BEATRICE OXFORD and HERBERT WINCHELL are:

16. i. VICKY LYNN[5] WINCHELL, b. October 1957. d. August 05, 1988
ii. TERRY LYNN WINCHELL, b. Bet. 1958 - 1959; m. GARY ALAN SIPOS.

10. JAMES RAY OXFORD[4] JR. *(JAMES RAY[3] OXFORD, SR, JAMES OLIVER[2], WILLIAM[1])* was born March 18, 1929. He married ROSALIND PATRICIA BOLES June 25, 1953.

Children of JAMES JR. and ROSALIND BOLES are:

i. MARRETHIA ANN[5] OXFORD, b. October 16, 1954.
ii. IDA LOUISE OXFORD, b. February 07, 1956. d. December 27, 1989
iii. PATRICIA LYNN OXFORD, b. January 05, 1967.

11. PAUL[4] OXFORD *(SAMUEL[3], JAMES OLIVER[2], WILLIAM[1])*. He married ENICE OXFORD in Pennington Gap, Virginia.

Children of PAUL OXFORD and ENICE OXFORD are:

i. EDWARD EUGENE[5] OXFORD.
ii. CHARLES WESLEY OXFORD.
iii. PAUL JR OXFORD.
iv. VIRGINIA MAELAWSON OXFORD.

Generation No. 5

12. CLARENCE KING MOREFIELD[5] JR *(GERALDINE[4] OXFORD, JAMES RAY[3], JAMES OLIVER[2], WILLIAM[1])* was born February 13, 1944 in Idaho. He married LORETTA LOWE November 13, 1965.

Children of CLARENCE JR and LORETTA LOWE are:
19. i. CLARENCE KING[6] MOREFIELD III, b. May 26, 1966.
20. ii. THERESA KAY MOREFIELD, b. April 23, 1969.

13. JOHN RUSSELL[5] MOREFIELD *(GERALDINE[4] OXFORD, JAMES RAY[3], JAMES OLIVER[2], WILLIAM[1])* was born August 26, 1946 in Jenkins, Kentucky. He married HEATHER GAY METCALF December 17, 1977.

Children of JOHN MOREFIELD and HEATHER METCALF are:
i. JESSE JAMES[6] MOREFIELD, b. June 20, 1980.
ii. RUTH ANN MOREFIELD, b. October 24, 1981.
iii. MICHELLE LYNN MOREFIELD, b. August 11, 1983.
iv. MAXWELL KAYHILL MOREFIELD, b. November 26, 1986.

14. SHARON KAY[5] MOREFIELD *(GERALDINE[4] OXFORD, JAMES RAY[3], JAMES OLIVER[2], WILLIAM[1])* was born September 19, 1957 in Detroit, MI. She married (1) RONALD ALLAN SMITH SR September 28, 1973 in Monroe, Mi, son of ROBERT SMITH and BETTY SOLEAU. She married (2) CLIFTON PAUL HARRIS September 17, 1983 in Coral Castle, Homestead, FL, son of LEWIS HARRIS and GLADYS REDDIN. She married (3) James Harold Powers on April 9, 2004 in Castle Rock, Colorado, the son of Charles Powers and Valeda Howell, he is a highly decorated retired Master Sergeant (E7) serving 20 years in the United States Air Force, during the Vietnam and Desert Storm wars.

Children of SHARON KAY MOREFIELD and RONALD SR are:
i. RONALD ALLAN SMITH[6] JR, b. June 28, 1974.
ii. BOBBIE JO SMITH, b. June 21, 1975.

15. CONSTANCE[5] STAJDA *(GLORIA ANN[4] OXFORD, JAMES RAY[3], JAMES OLIVER[2], WILLIAM[1])* was born November 22, 1963. She married (1) TIMOTHY ALAN LEBLANC August 28, 1981 in Divorced in May of 1983. She married (2) JAMES CHARLES REEVES JR August 15, 1986.

Child of CONSTANCE STAJDA and TIMOTHY LEBLANC is:

i. TRAVIS MICHAEL^{6} LEBLANC, b. February 22, 1982.

Children of CONSTANCE STAJDA and JAMES JR are:

ii. JAMES CHARLES^{6} REEVES III, b. March 12, 1988.

iii. MACK ALEXANDER REEVES, b. May 22, 1993.

iv. TRAVIS MICHAEL LEBLANC REEVES, b. February 22, 1982.

More About TRAVIS MICHAEL LEBLANC REEVES:

Adoption: May 1990

16. VICKY LYNN^{5} WINCHELL *(BEATRICE LORINE^{4} OXFORD, JAMES RAY^{3}, JAMES OLIVER^{2}, WILLIAM^{1})* was born October 1957. She married SCOTT FOLLBAUM 1975.

Children of VICKY WINCHELL and SCOTT FOLLBAUM are:

i. ERIN^{6} FOLLBAUM, b. February 15, 1977.

ii. DEVON FOLLBAUM, b. September 30, 1979.

Generation No. 6

17. CLARENCE KING^{6} MOREFIELD III *(CLARENCE KING MOREFIELD^{5} JR, GERALDINE^{4} OXFORD, JAMES RAY^{3}, JAMES OLIVER^{2}, WILLIAM^{1})* was born May 26, 1966.

Child of CLARENCE KING MOREFIELD III is:

i. ETHAN^{7} MOREFIELD.

18. THERESA KAY^{6} MOREFIELD *(CLARENCE KING MOREFIELD^{5} JR, GERALDINE^{4} OXFORD, JAMES RAY^{3}, JAMES OLIVER^{2}, WILLIAM^{1})* was born April 23, 1969. She married CRAIG PATCH February 14, 1990.

Children of THERESA MOREFIELD and CRAIG PATCH are:

i. JOSHUA^{7} PATCH.

ii. JACOB ^{7} PATCH.

19. RONALD ALLAN ^{6} SMITH - *(SHARON KAY^{5} MOREFIELD, GERALDINE^{4} OXFORD, JAMES RAY^{3}, JAMES OLIVER^{2}, WILLIAM^{1})* was born June 28, 1974 in Monroe, MI. He met CINDI THERESA CLICK in Winfield High School, Winfield, MO. (1) married AMY JONES on September 17, 2000.

Children of RONALD SMITH and CINDI CLICK are:

i. BRIAN ALLAN^{7} SMITH, b. Troy, MO.

ii. MARCUS ANTHONY ^{7} SMITH, b. Troy, MO.

Children of RONALD SMITH and AMY JONES are:

i. GABRIELLE MARIE [7] SMITH, b. June 2, 2001 in St. Louis, Mo.
ii. RONALD ALLAN [7] SMITH III, b. June 22, 2003 in St. Louis, Mo.

20. BOBBIE JO [6] SMITH - *(SHARON KAY[5] MOREFIELD, GERALDINE[4] OXFORD, JAMES RAY[3], JAMES OLIVER[2], WILLIAM[1])* was born June 21, 1975 in Monroe, MI. She is common law married to RONNIE GONZ in St. Peters, MO.

Children of BOBBIE SMITH and RONNIE GONZ is:

i. TASIA JO[7] GONZ, b. April 11, 1998, Barnes Jewish Hospital, St. Peters, MO.
ii. AUSTIN[7] JOE GONZ, b. September 26, 2004

21. RUTH ANN [6] MOREFIELD (JOHN RUSSELL[5] MOREFIELD, *GERALDINE[4] OXFORD, JAMES RAY[3], JAMES OLIVER[2], WILLIAM[1])*was born October 24, 1981 \, married GARY DAVID WHITEHOUSE on October 14, 2007 in Monroe, MI.

Children of RUTH ANN MOREFIELD and GARY DAVID WHITEHOUSE are:

i. AVA JOY[7] WHITEHOUSE, b. May 27, 2006 in Monroe, MI.
ii. GARY DAVID [7] WHITEHOUSE JR., b. February 23, 2008 in Monroe, MI.

22. MICHELLE LYNN[6] MOREFIELD, (JOHN RUSSELL [5] MOREFIELD, GERALDINE [4] OXFORD, JAMES RAY [3], JAMES OLIVER [2], WILLIAM [1]) born August 11, 1983.

Child of MICHELLE LYNN MOREFIELD is:

i. MILES JAMES [7] MCBRIDE, born August 24, 2007 in Monroe, MI.

Printed in the United States
139082LV00010BA/46/P